50
Feminist
Art Manifestos

Edited by Katy Deepwell

KT press publishes books and *n.paradoxa: international feminist art journal* to promote understanding of women artists and their work

50 Feminist Art Manifestos
Katy Deepwell (editor)

ISBN: 978-0-9926934-6-6

EPUB: ISBN: 978-0-9926934-5-9

An earlier version of this book was published as an .epub, *Feminist Art Manifestos: An Anthology,* KT press, 2014. ISBN: 978-0-9926934-3-5

Publisher: KT press, 38 Bellot Street, London, SE10 0AQ, UK
Website: https://www.ktpress.co.uk

Book series editor: Katy Deepwell
To report errors, please email: ktpress@ktpress.co.uk

Every effort was made to contact all copyright holders, if there are any errors or omissions to the captions or credits, please inform the publishers of the oversight. The publisher has no responsibility for the persistence or accuracy of the URLs for any external or third party internet websites referred to in this book and does not guarantee that any content on such websites is or will remain accurate or appropriate.

1. Theory of art: Contemporary art 2. Feminist theory 3. Art Manifestos
I. Deepwell, Katy (editor). II. Title.

CONTENTS

Negotiations: Feminist Art Manifestos

Katy Deepwell

What is a manifesto? A political programme, a declaration, a definitive statement of belief. Neither institutional mission statement, nor religious dogma; neither a poem, nor a book. As a form of literature, manifestos occupy a specific place in the history of public discourse as a means to communicate radical ideas. Often distributed as ephemeral documents, as leaflets or pamphlets in political campaigns or as announcements of the formation of new parties or new avant-gardes, manifestos above all declare what its authors are for and against, and ask people who read them to join them, to understand, to share these ideas. The feminist art manifestos in this anthology have all of these attributes as they explore the potential and possibilities of women's cultural production as artists.

I first compiled a list of feminist manifestos for *n.paradoxa: international feminist art journal*'s website in preparation for a seminar I organised at the ICA in London in 2011. Many of these manifestos were available online, but not all: four of them I had published earlier in *n.paradoxa*. I started hunting for manifestos to add to the list and quickly found more that had been published or distributed but weren't well known or easily available. The ICA seminar was based on reading these manifestos collectively and out loud as I thought they should be spoken and shared/heard in a group rather than read quietly and alone. Bringing them together created an opportunity to discuss the changes within feminist cultural politics and different forms of feminist poetics over the last forty years. Different forms of relationships between feminist politics as a set of "demands" and feminist art practices and poetics are evident within these manifestos. They can also be read as experiments in feminist aesthetics focused on women artists' subjectivities, modes of expression and creative potential.

Arranging them into a chronological list underlined the fact that women artists had produced manifestos as early as 1965 and well beyond the women's liberation movement of the 1970s. Each manifesto presents distinct and specific qualities because of when they were written and how they express their ideas. While there has been an academic tendency to "confine" the politics of feminism and feminist art practices to the 1970s or to an Anglo-American dynamic, this collection reveals that this was not the case. Reading across these manifestos makes the shifting paths within feminism visible, paths which demonstrate what the movement has represented to artists working in many different parts of the world since the late 1960s. The chronological order aims to encourage readers to consider this history, because it demonstrates that feminist histories are not a simple linear development or progression. Like *n.paradoxa*, which I founded and edited 1998-2017, this selection affirms the broad international dynamic to what has been achieved over the last fifty years of feminisms as well as highlights the very different threads of enquiries and challenges made. The first collection I published as an ebook by KT press in 2014, with 35 manifestos. This volume contains 50, and although it is extensive, it is not comprehensive. Those published elsewhere are listed in the bibliography, including several book length manifestos.

This collection concentrates on manifestos which are about feminist art production and film-making by feminist artists. I felt that a separate collection on feminist art manifestos was necessary as all too often the same three or four feminist manifestos are reproduced in manifesto collections or anthologies of artists' writings. The most famous, even infamous, and widely reproduced is Valerie Solanas' SCUM manifesto, which I took the decision not to seek to reproduce as it is widely available in print and online, similarly Donna Haraway's 'Manifesto for Cyborgs' which is also widely reproduced. Two more recent manifestos, *Glitch Feminism* and *Xenofeminism* have been published as books. All the manifestos here are published in full. When I first compiled the manifesto list online in 2010, I linked these art manifestos with many other early feminist political manifestos from anarchist, radical separatist, left-wing and red stocking political groups, as well as some early feminist and futurist manifestos from the 1910s. A closer examination of the relationship between the politics of art and the politics of feminism is what I hope this volume will provoke. I also set up in May 2020, a mass open online course (MOOC) on Feminist Art Manifestos at nparadoxa.com as well as running different reading seminars with students in London, Prague and Malmo.

I was inspired by Janet Lyons' book on manifestos, *Provocations of the Modern*, which does not avoid discussing the poetics and politics of feminism and offers many very insights into how manifestos frame their arguments. Her chosen contemporary feminist examples were Jenny Holzer's multi-media work *Truisms* (which has been fly-posters, a wall-work, T-shirts, as well as an artwork presented in LED displays in public spaces and large scale outdoor light projections 1977-present) and the manifestos and handbooks of The Lesbian Avengers from the 1990s. Through these examples, Lyons draws a relationship between early avant-garde politics, poetics and contemporary feminism.

It is important to emphasise that in this collection, these texts are not identical in approach, content or poetics. They arise from different historical moments and locations and each expresses widely divergent political views. If they share anything, it could only be defined very loosely by a common concern for women's art practices, feminist politics and women's creative potential as artists. The writing embraces many different kinds of poetics, modes of address and values as well as pursuing different topics from care, love and sexuality, to witchcraft and cyberfeminism, from aspirations for the future to ideas about directions for future creative works (known and unknown).

If a manifesto is a political declaration or a statement for and against certain positions, tendencies and beliefs, then what is being declared in this collection? The last fifty years have witnessed an explosion of different forms of feminism from the early politics of women's liberation – which was itself a very broad alliance of different social, cultural and political groupings – to calls for affirmative action; to campaigns for equal opportunities in cultural politics; to ecofeminisms; to cyberfeminisms; to lesbian feminisms; to Afro-futurist feminisms; to calls for new forms of solidarity or alliance in inter-sectional and political formations. Feminism is a dynamic politics and the singularity of this term has always covered a broad range of political opinions: liberal, left-wing, right-wing, radical, anarchist, separatist, cyberfeminist and eco-feminist. Nevertheless, feminism has been resolutely anti-sexist, anti-racist, anti-homophobic, anti-ageist, anti-capitalist and anti-Imperalist. Within these texts the feminist arguments include calls for separatism (in women's publications, groups and exhibitions), for wider recognition of women's cultural production, for new forms of collaboration between women in cultural politics and for collective action by women to demand change.

Most of these texts offer different critiques of the status quo, of how to think about patriarchy/capitalism/colonialism and currently proscribed roles for men and women in our society, and these differences may come as a surprise to many. However, they often state that there remains a limited, dismissive view of the woman artist locally and globally. Against this negative position and the stereotyping or stigmatising view of both femininity and female creativity, each proceeds to announce and affirm what women's creativity has been, is and might become given the current cultural and political situation. As well as analysis, there is much utopian thinking in these declarations. These manifestos importantly open a space for the future of women's creative art practices – without filling it with any single didactic programme. Where they do announce a programme or a broader scope for future work they affirm a new and creative beginning of what might be possible for women artists, for art and for feminist politics.

Manifestos were one of the principal documents through which the avant-gardes of the early twentieth century announced their artistic position, and they are routinely republished and studied as a feature of pre-war avant-garde art practices, especially those around the modern art movements of Dadaism, Futurism and Surrealism. Women's contributions to this modernist genre are often overlooked, especially the early manifestos of Valentine de Saint Point and Mina Loy. Collections of artists' writings post-war have stood in for the manifesto in late modern and contemporary art alongside the idea that a mission statement announcing an artists' group is also a manifesto. Feminism has had its own internal debates about whether it is an avant-garde movement post-1968 in the field of contemporary art or not and this is a question about whether it exhibits avant-gardism in the cultural politics of art practices or should be considered instead in terms of a more broadly conceived politics of cultural interventions and change in society. This is because feminism is not an art style, a brand, a fashion trend or a recognisable artistic category known as "women's art" or "feminist art", nor is it centred around images of "the body" aka "women's bodies". There are many who have argued against forms of avant-gardism within feminism (regarding what was the women's art movement as a broad collective movement and refuting any conception of a unified style or set of concerns). Others have advanced the argument that any feminist cultural politics represents a strong critique of the historical avant-garde, its politics and tactics or ways of politically organising resistance and this is why feminism cannot be considered an avant-garde, even as an alternative. Some, however, do regard feminism as the last true avant-garde movement in the twentieth century. Insofar as the manifestos in this book indicate differences between women historically and politically, this anthology confirms the complexity of these historical relations and political questions about feminism as an avant-garde.

Within the anthology, there are many references to earlier manifestos in terms of the writing style used and in how a position is declared. Arahmaiani's 'Letter to Marinetti', for example, references the style of his Futurist manifesto; Mette Ingvartsen's 'Yes Manifesto' operates a deliberate inversion of Rainer's 'No Manifesto' and the 100 Anti-theses of the Old Boys Network cyberfeminist Manifesto aims to be as rhetorical and controversial as Martin Luther's ninety-five 'Theses on Religion'. Remedes' 'S.C.U.B. manifesto' echoes Valerie Solanas' SCUM Manifesto, which begins with the sentence:

> 'Life in this society being, at best, an utter bore and no aspect of society being at all relevant to women, there remains to civic-minded, responsible, thrill-seeking females only to overthrow the government, eliminate the money system, institute complete automation, and destroy the male sex.'

While Solanas' position on destruction of the male sex is not advocated by any of these manifestos, their critique of patriarchy is inseparable from a feminist vision for the future. Patriarchy is analysed in many different terms across the anthology: it is not simply men against women nor is feminism here the sexist caricature of it as seeking an inverted society where women take precedence over men. While the specific term "oppression" arises in the art manifestos from the 1970s, the critique of patriarchy as a social system and a way of thinking which privileges men over women in society runs throughout these texts. Feminists argue that patriarchy is a system of social organisation which has produced women's oppression as a group, suppressed women's knowledge and former culture (not always conceived as a matriarchy), reinforced the exploitation of women in capitalism as second-class and low-paid waged labourers and failed to recognise their value as unwaged workers (as mothers and carers). Patriarchy, as both a social system and a way of thinking, has over-determined the position of women in art, in culture, in capitalism, in colonialism/Imperialism and in globalisation and produced the objectification of women in mass media, as bodies seen and not heard or, as Rita Mae Brown puts it, polarised as either 'nostalgia' or 'porno-violence'. With the rise of different forms of identity politics and the critique of essentialist thinking within feminism from the late 1970s onwards, feminists have used the term "oppression" less often, but when they do they are referring back to this critique of patriarchy and how women's position in society is over-determined by misogynist thinking about women. Gisela Breitling in 1989, for example, describes the myths of patriarchy as a form of "Club Law", while Alexandra Pirici and Raluca Voinea, in 2015, argue for capitalism's and patriarchy's overthrow in their vision of an alternative 'Gynecene'.

Feminist analysis of patriarchy has led women to many different forms of analysis about the position of women in relation to the state and religion. These manifestos speak about a political defence of the earth (Stephens and Sprinkle) and the weak (Factory of Found Clothes/Gluklya) and the vulnerable exploited by capitalism, by globalisation, by sexism, by heterosexism, by racism, classism, ageism and by imperialism. Feminism's agenda for social change has been about the transformation of what it means to be human and that is a cultural move beyond calls for social justice or equality before the law in a campaign. This means changing the lives of both men and women in our society by escaping all proscribed or stereotyped roles that have predetermined a woman's destiny. Feminism here reaches beyond specific agendas in legal, social and civil rights for women, to recognise how practices in everyday life, in cultural representations and in the representation of women as cultural producers reinforce sexist thought and practice. Many of these texts affirm women's rights as human rights and point to the fact that without women's rights, there is no meaningful conception of human rights: see the manifestos by Arahmaiani or Women Artists of Pakistan and Yes Association! or the Permanent Assembly of Women Art Workers for different approaches to this.

These manifestos offer new and distinct views of what women artists' creativity will consist of in the future: see, for example, Carolee Schneemann's 'Woman in the Year 2000' (1974). Berg and Sjöö's rejection of middle-class mores and the dominant culture of abstraction in the galleries of the 1970s is accompanied by the question: 'HOW DOES ONE COMMUNICATE WOMEN'S STRENGTH, STRUGGLE, RISING UP FROM OPPRESSION, BLOOD, CHILDBIRTH, SEXUALITY?' Even if we cannot predict what women will produce in the future we do know that, if their contribution is recognised, if their education is transformed, they will produce something unexpected, different and positive in its own terms, as stated in VALIE EXPORT's 'Woman's Art' or 'Women Artists of Pakistan'. Maria Klonaris and Katerina Thomadaki argue for 'an other cinema' in their manifesto that is simultaneously a claim for women's autonomy, for independent thinking and creation, and a new form of cinema removed from the fantastic projections about women's culture or "otherness" written about or understood by men. SubRosa advance a 'post-modern commons', a space for new forms of hybridity and possibility to emerge in 'REFUGIA', while Julie Perini outlines her philosophy for a new form of relational film-making between director and subject, in both process and result.

Manifestos are often considered ephemeral documents; some circulate only as flyers, posters, press-releases or web pages. In this anthology, a few of these manifestos were produced as artworks (for example, Dora Garcia and Anneta Mona Chisa / Lucia Tkáčová) and Ewa Partum and Yes Association!'s statements developed from or as texts spoken in performances. The language of speech, of declaration and of performance is present in, for example, Silvia Ziranek, and of poetry and aphorisms in Agnes Denes or Lily Bea Moor (aka Senga Nengudi). Some of these statements existed as catalogue essays or announcements such as ORLAN, Elke Krystufek or Violetta Liagatchev. Other manifestos have circulated exclusively on the web, like the work of VNS Matrix or Stephen and Sprinkle.

Many kinds of poetics emerge in how these different documents are written, but it is notable how frequently repetition, bullet points or lists are used to express the complexity and multiplicity of position. The most concise is the most collectively authored, the 'Ongoing Womanifesto' from 1975, approved and signed by 80 women. Reversal, irony or humour are often strategically deployed in these manifestos, see VNS Matrix or The Guerrilla Girls or Tkacova and Chisa, for example. A position is affirmed even when the manifesto itself states only negative terms or a list of refusals, as in the Old Boys Network's 'Anti-theses'. What might become possible is affirmed by listing impossibilities, as in Dora Garcia's text, or a long list of what feminism is not, evident in the 'First Manifesto on the Cultural Revolution of Women' or 'No, Nein, Niet!!!!'.

A manifesto remains the ultimate propaganda document announcing programmes for social or political change and condensing declarations of moral and political belief into graspable slogans. Such documents in political life are repeatedly produced and revised by political parties, including marginal and alternative groups, and their aspirations are increasingly echoed in the mission statements of NGOs. Although I came across some very interesting founding statements of feminist art groups – from the Sirens group in China as they launched their gallery/ studio in the 1990s, or Pecha Blenda in the 2010s, or La Sal in Spain in the 1970s – these were more often programmatic mission statements rather than manifestos. The Feminist Art Gallery in Toronto's slogan, produced as an artwork in crochet, was 'WE CAN'T COMPETE/WE WON'T COMPETE / WE CAN'T KEEP UP/ WE WON'T KEEP DOWN', words which echo Kate Walker's manifesto on the rejection of competition as important to the project *Feministo*.

Women artists' groups have been numerous in the second half of the twentieth century and into the twenty-first century and many have produced statements at the time of an exhibition or in publications. In this bureaucratic age, the need to declare what you are about and what you represent in a mission statement is however distinct as a mode of address from the appeal of a manifesto which encourages people to subscribe to your ideas. The few founding statements are included because they attempted to signal a new type of politics (see Feminist Art Action Brigade (FAAB), Factory of Found Clothes (FFC), Lenka Clayton's Artists' Residency in Motherhood, Not Surprised or Nosotras Propemos) even when some of these alliances ultimately proved to be temporary. In the case of Eva and Co., ironically their manifesto announces the dissolution of their group, but its list of refusals to be co-opted as yet another artists' group within the art world signal the difficulties of keeping going – in terms of the life-span of a group and competing commitments – even when relative success as an organisation is achieved.

Many feminist manifestos from Mina Loy to Carla Lonzi have warned that feminism has never been only about equality and that believing feminism will end when some form of equality in numbers has been reached is an illusion which will not change sexism or patriarchal thinking. Like these two writers, many of the feminists here question whether equality between the sexes is feminism's only or ultimate goal (see ARCO manifesto or No, Nein, Niet!!!!!). Nevertheless, several of these manifestos refer to how quotas will be necessary to change the representation of women artists in our exhibitions and museums. Women artists are not a minority amongst all artists. They are seen as a minority group only because of the selection procedures of exhibitions and the practices of criticism and art history where gender remains a decisive, often unacknowledged, factor in how discrimination operates. Too often discussion of gender (which is both male / female, masculinity / femininity) is sidelined and regarded as irrelevant to the processes of the selective tradition, which filter and discriminate to turn the many into the few, or in the collecting practices of museums and collectors who feed off this knowledge in their pursuit of "the best". WSABAL's statement in 1970 was incredibly radical and forward-thinking in its insistence on levels of representation for women and particularly for black women artists in open exhibitions in New York. Its distribution sparked debate: it was a provocation and a call to action. Many have followed this attempt to represent women artists at levels appropriate to their existence in the population (52%) and to insist on representation according to population, including all ethnic minorities and religious minorities. As Lily Bea Moor writes 'We do in deed E X I S T' and the same critique arises in more detail in Chila Kumari Burman's essay 'Why have there been no great black women artists?' (1987) which took up the question Linda Nochlin raised in 1971 and turns it to an analysis of the discrimination against women artists from ethnic minorities in the UK, particularly in art schools. In Sweden, which many regard as a model for social democratic practices which uphold equality between the sexes, Yes! Association's agreement was prompted and facilitated by the opening of a feminist exhibition at which the group presented a detailed analysis of institutionalised discrimination in museums against women artists. Included here is their original text and their attempt to apply these rules to the Brooklyn Museum a few years later. Utilising the language of contract law, their Equal Opportunities Agreement was an attempt for an instition to make a commitment to reviewing equal opportunities indefinitely into the future. However, can the unequal representation of women artists be easily and objectively measured by a change in numbers between the sexes? As Silvia Ziranek states, is what we really need: 'MORE QUALITY THROUGH FEMALE QUANTITY'. The ARCO manifesto (2005) arose in a very different moment in a series of public debates about feminism held in a large talks programme at the ARCO art fair in Madrid. As such, it was directed at museum directors' and collectors' acquisition policies. By repeating the Guerrilla Girls early poster: 'What will your collection be worth when sexism and racism are no longer fashionable?', it too acted as a provocation for future work and was signed by many leading feminist curators and art historians in Europe and the USA. In 2017/2018, Nosotras Propemos; We are Not Surprised; and the people behind the 'Code for a Feminist (Art) Institution' and 'No, Nein, Niet!!!!' manifestos offer many other distinct propositions for changing the situation of women artists internationally. These approaches are worth contrasting with earlier texts like Berg and Sjöö which in the 1970s questioned whether the gallery system would ever provide recognition for women given the marked discrimination against them.

Representation in numerical strength is only one part of countering discrimination and injustices in distribution of wealth and of goods: as political philosopher Nancy Fraser has argued, recognition is also key. Chisa and Tkáčová's text, by contrast, produced by two women artists invited to represent their country in a biennale, wittily weighs up what this stake in national representation will mean for them and their work as emerging artists. they chose to use Pareto's 80/20 principle precisely because a just balance of 50/50 does not exist. Recognition for the work that women do and the value of that work arises again and again in this anthology. The tension between development and maintenance is central to Mierle Laderman Ukeles' 'Manifesto for Maintenance Art'. Maintenance work is often thought of as invisible, repetitive and unrewarding. It is even conceived of as the antithesis to art, where this is held up to be the epitome of free intellectual labour determined by a creative individual. Ukeles' radical reconsideration of economics and ecology, literally how we deal with questions of our production and waste and what is cared for or disregarded in our society, transformed this maintenance labour into Art. Reproduction of the conditions for production in unwaged labour is frequently neglected in political and economic debates which remain focused on production of goods and waged labour, even in the service sector. Women's labour patterns have changed in the new service-based economies and in globalised domestic markets since the 1960s. However, women's role in reproduction – through motherhood, care for the sick and elderly, in the extended family and in voluntary work for the vulnerable, the community or in education and civil society – still regularly disappears from view in public debates about what work means and how it is valued. Withdrawing this reproductive, developmental and maintenance labour would bring capitalism to its knees, because it has been so fundamental to its continuation. From this analysis of the devaluation of unwaged labour came the idea women should go on strike and withdraw from housework or any further investment in a system which discriminates against them, (Wages for Housework campaigns are another response to this). The irony of 'Doing Nothing' as a form of resistance to capitalism's advance over every aspect of everyday life is embraced by niichegodelat: while, as Linda Mary Montano, suggests we need to rethink our attachment to the economy of money.

The work of education is referred to in many of these manifestos as a positive force for change in women's opportunities, even though discrimination persists. The potential to offer different curricula and a different set of values has been at the heart of feminist teaching, a new i-story for women as Schneemann suggests. Budapest, Rosenbach and Coven's manifesto looks back to matriarchy, to magic for an affirmation of a different kind of value system for feminism. The persecution of witches became a symbol for modern feminists of the persecution of women's traditions and the suppression of their knowledge by the modern church and state in patriarchal forms of religious practice, where men came to hold authority over the congregation. As they suggest: 'when we are fighting for the right to control our own bodies, it is also time to fight for the well-being of our souls.' The right to fight all forms of superstition, cant and prejudice is also reaffirmed in the Women Artists of Pakistan Manifesto alongside the need to 'respect and uphold the right of every woman artist to her own faith, her individual approach to content, form, medium, method, technique and style in the realisation of her artistic ideals'. The FAAC's collective's statement shows how the precarious and differential position of women lecturers is now thought in intersectional and internationalist ways as well as a set of commitments made to challenging existing patterns of thought.

The continued importance of feminism, in different contexts and forms of collective feminist cultural politics, is affirmed in the production of each of these manifestos. The imagination, reinvention and affirmation visible in these texts is the most optimistic message in these manifestos and why they should be known more widely and read as inspiration and encouragement to artists everywhere.

This anthology was only made possible by the generous agreement of all the authors/ artists who shared the understanding that collecting together and distributing these manifestos would prove worthwhile to renew, reconsider and continue feminist cultural politics in the future. I want to thank them for their work. Special thanks to Nancy Hynes, Daisy Lafarge and Celia Lacey for their help in preparing the first edition of 35 manifestos as an ebook in 2014 and Silvia Ziranek for proofing this text.

Bibliography - On manifestos

Umbro Apollonio *Futurist Manifestos* (Tate Publishing, Limited, 2009)

Umbro Apollonio (ed. and introduction) translated from Italian: Robert Brain, afterword by Richard Humphreys. *Futurist manifestos* (Boston, Mass: MFA, 2001)

Craig Buckley (ed.) *After the Manifesto* (Published by GSAPP/T6 Ediciones)

Cambridge Literary Review On Manifestos, 11 (2018)

Mary Ann Caws (ed.) *Manifesto: a century of isms* (Lincoln, Neb. ; London : University of Nebraska Press, 2001)

Laura Cull and Will Daddario *Manifesto Now! Instructions for Performance, Philosophy, Politics* (Intellect, 2013)

Alex Danchev (ed. and introduction) *100 artists' manifestos* (London: Penguin, 2011)

Caroline Gausden 'Feminist manifesto and social art practice archive'. [Website based on thesis, 2016]. http://feministmanifesto.co.uk/index.html

Breanne Fahs (ed.) *Burn It Down!: Feminist Manifestos for the Revolution* (Verso, 2020)

Julian Hanna *The Manifesto Handbook: 95 Theses on an Incendiary Form* (Zero Books, 2019)

Jessica Lack *Why are we 'artists'? : 100 world art manifestos* London : Penguin Classics, 2017.

Nicola Lees, Hans Ulrich Obrist, Julia Peyton-Jones *Serpentine Gallery Manifesto Marathon* (Koenig Books, 2009).

Janet Lyons *Manifestoes: Provocations of the Modern* (Cornell University Press, 1999)

Scott MacKenzie (ed.) *Film Manifestos and Global Cinema Cultures: A Critical Anthology* (Univ of California Press, 2014)

Bob Osborn *Understanding Futurism through its Manifestos* (wbdpublications, ebook)

Michalis Pichler (ed.) *Publishing Manifestos: An International Anthology* (MIT, 2019)

Luca Somigli *Legitimizing the Artist: Manifesto Writing and European Modernism, 1885-*

1915 (University of Toronto Press, 2003)

Carlota Subirós (dir.) *GRRRLS!!! Manifestos feministes del segle XX i XXI (20th And 21st Century Feminist Manifestos)* (a film, 2019)

Suffragette Manifestos (Penguin Great Ideas, 2020)

Penny A. Weiss (ed.) *Feminist Manifestos: A Global Documentary Reader* (New York University Press, 2018)

Burcu Dogramaci and Katja Schneider (Hg.) *Clear the air: Künstler-Manifeste seit den 1960er Jahren* (Bielefeld: transcript, Edition Kulturwissenschaft, 2017)

Laura Winkiel *Modernism, race, and manifestos* (Cambridge University Press, 2008)

Feminist (Art) Manifestos (not included in this book)

Valentine de Saint Point 'The Manifesto of Futurist Woman (Response to F. T. Marinetti)' (1912)

Valentine de Saint Point 'Futurist Manifesto of Lust' (11 Jan 1913)

Mina Loy 'Feminist Manifesto' (1914) published in Roger L. Conover (ed.) *The Lost Lunar Baedeker: Poems of Mina Loy* (Carcanet, 1985; Farrar, Straus and Giroux, 1997).

Valerie Solanas *SCUM manifesto* (1969) (London : Phoenix Press, 1991)

The Radical Women Manifesto: Socialist Feminist Theory, Program, and Organizational Structure (1967) (Red Letter Press, 2001)

'Redstockings Manifesto' (1969/1970). 'The Redstockings Manifesto' was used by the Women's Liberation Party in 1969.

Monique Wittig, Gilles Wittig, Marcia Rothenberg and Margaret Stephenson 'Combat pour la liberation del a femme' *L'Idiot International* (Paris) May 1970 pp.12-16

Black Woman's Manifesto (1970) (a pamphlet by Third World Women's Alliance in New York, archived in Duke University Library)

Chicago Anarcho-Feminists 'Anarcho-Feminism: Two Statements' (from *Siren*, 1971) 'Who we are: An Anarcho-Feminist Manifesto' and 'Blood Of The Flower: An Anarchist-Feminist Statement'

Demands from the National Women's Liberation Movement conferences (1971-1978)(UK). Archived on the Feminist Archive North website.

Jo Freeman *The BITCH Manifesto* (1972): An analysis of how strong independent women are viewed in our society. Archived on Chicago Women's Liberation Union Archive website.

Carla Lonzi *Let's Spit on Hegel* (Rivolta Femminile). Translated to English by Veronica Newman (New York: Secunda, 2010)

'The Artists' Union: 'Women's Workshop Manifesto'' (Almost Free Theatre, London 1973) reproduced in Hilary Robinson (ed.) *Feminism-Art-Theory* (Blackwells, 2001)

Donna Haraway 'Manifesto for Cyborgs' (1985) First published in *Socialist Review* No 80 1985. Reprinted in Linda Nicholson (ed.) *Feminism/Postmodernism* (Routledge, 1991) and republished in Amelia Jones (ed.) *The Feminism and Visual Culture Reader* (London: Routledge, 2003).

Lesbian Avengers of New York Civil Organising Project *Out Against Right: The Dyke Manifesto: basic principles* (1992-1994)

Mary Daly *Quintessence- realizing the archaic future : a radical elemental feminist manifesto* (Boston: Beacon press, 1998)

Beatriz Preciado *Manifeste contrasexuel/Contrasexual Manifesto*. Also known as *Manifiesto contra-sexual/Kontrasexuelles Manifest* (Paris: Editions Ballard, 2000)

Lida Sherafatmand 'Humanitarian Art Manifesto' (2004-2010) (published online, 30 Sept 2010, Kimpavitapress)

'East German Feminists: Lila Manifesto' *Feminist Studies* vol.16 (Fall 1990) pp.621-634

Natasha Vita-More 'Extropic Art Manifesto of Transhumanist Arts' (1997)

Meike Schmidt-Gleim and Mieke Verloo 'ONE MORE FEMINIST MANIFESTO OF THE POLITICAL' *IWM Working Paper* No. 2/2003 (Vienna, 2003)

'Manifesto of the Pan-Canadian Young Feminist Gathering Toujours: RebELLEs / Waves of Resistance' (Montreal, October 13, 2008).

Lindsey German 'A Feminist Manifesto for the 21st Century' (2010) Eclectics blogartine

Martine Syms 'Mundane Afro-futurist Manifesto' (2013) Rhizome.org (17 Dec 2013)

Laboria Cuboniks *The Xenofeminist Manifesto: A Politics for Alienation* (Verso, 2018)

Cinzia Arruzza, Tithi Bhattacharya and Nancy Fraser *Feminism for the 99%: A Manifesto* (Verso, 2019)

Legacy Russell 'Digital Dualism and the Glitch Manifesto' (2012), The Society Pages.org and article on Rhizome.org, 2013. Legacy Russell *Glitch Feminism Manifesto* ([2013]; Verso, 2020)

FemTechNet Manifesto (2013) https://femtechnet.org/publications/manifesto/

Anohni - Kembra Pfahler - Johanna Constantine - Bianca Casady - Sierra Casady 'the-13-tenets-of-future-feminism (2014-2017)' published online.

Laura Bear, Karen Ho, Anna Lowenhaupt Tsing, and Sylvia Yanagisako *Gens: A Feminist Manifesto for the Study of Capitalism* (2015). Published in *Cultural Anthropology*

Miriam E. David *A Feminist Manifesto for Education* (Wiley, 2016)

Lina Džuverović, Irene Revell "We falter with feminist conviction": Notes on Assumptions, Expectations, Confidence, and Doubt in the Feminist Art Organisation' *On Curating* Issue 29/May 2016 *Curating in Feminist Thought*.

'The Feminists are Cackling in the Archive' *Feminist Review* vol.115/1(2016) pp.155-164

Chimamanda Ngozi Adichie *Dear Ijeawele, or A Feminist Manifesto in Fifteen Suggestions* (Penguin, Random House, 2017)

Lena Šimic 'Manifesto for Maternal Performance (Art) 2016!' *Performance research.*Vol. 22/ 4 (2017), pp 131-139

Sara Ahmed 'A Killjoy Manifesto' in *Living a Feminist Life* (Duke University Press,2017)

Neysa Page-Lieberman and Melissa Hilliard Potter 'Feminist Social Practice: A Manifesto' *ASPA Journal* (John Hopkins Unversity Press) Vol. 3, no. 2, May 2018, pp.335-351

Jana Astanov 'An Astrofeminist Manifesto' (2018) Published online on creatrixmag.com.

Care collective *The Care Manifesto: The Politics of Interdependence: The Politics of Compassion* (Verso, 2020)

Additional Notes on manifestos in this book

1. **Yvonne Rainer - 'No Manifesto' (1965) - 'A Manifesto Reconsidered' (2008)**
   The 'No manifesto' was first published as one paragraph in Rainer's essay: 'Some retrospective notes on a dance for 10 people and 12 mattresses called "Parts of Some Sextets", performed at the Wadsworth Atheneum, Hartford, Connecticut, and Judson Memorial Church, New York, in March, 1965', *Tulane Drama Review* Vol. 10, No. 2 (Winter 1965). In her book, *Feelings are Facts*, Yvonne Rainer wrote 'that infamous "NO manifesto" has dogged my heels ever since it was first published….It was never meant to be prescriptive for all time for all choreographers, but rather, to do what the time honored tradition of the manifesto always intended manifestos to do; clear the air at a particular cultural and historical moment' (*Feelings are Facts: A Life* (MIT, 2006) p. 264). In her 1965 essay, she had specified in 'Postscript. 3. All I am inclined to indicate here are various feelings about *Parts of Some Sextets* and its effort in a certain direction - an area of concern as yet not fully clarified for me in relation to dance, but existing as a very large NO to many facts in the theatre today. (This is not to say that I personally do not enjoy many forms of theatre. It is only to define more stringently the rules and boundaries of my own artistic game of the moment.)' *Tulane Drama Review* (1965) pp.177-178. 'A Manifesto Reconsidered (2008)' was first published/ performed in 'The Manifesto Marathon' (Serpentine Gallery, London, 2008) and is the author's riposte to her own 'No Manifesto'. Copyright © Yvonne Rainer, reproduced with permission of the author.

2. **Mierle Laderman Ukeles - MANIFESTO FOR MAINTENANCE ART, 1969! Proposal for an exhibition: "CARE" (1969)**
   This version is taken from the text published on Ronald Feldman Gallery, New York website. Copyright © Mierle Laderman Ukeles. Courtesy of Ronald Feldman Fine Arts, New York and Artist. In an interview in *Art in America*, Ukeles states: 'In October 1969, in a cold fury, I sat down and I wrote the manifesto naming Maintenance Art. It arrived in one package though it was not the result of one simple idea as many people think, but of layers of causes which led up to this encapsulation. Art is often an encapsulation of a whole flow of things that end up in one formal thing, and the formal thing here was the manifesto document.' (18 March 2009). She began a series of *Private Performances of Personal Maintenance as Art* in 1970, documented as photographs. She took part in Lucy Lippard's exhibition, *c 7,500* (1973) with 4 performances at its second venue, Wadsworth Atheneum, *Washing/Tracks/ Maintenance: Outside*. The exhibition *CARE!* remained a proposal. This text was first reproduced in Lucy Lippard *Six Years: The Dematerialisation of the Art Object from 1966-1972* (New York: Praeger, 1973 and New York: New York University Press, 1979). Part I is reproduced in Kristine Stiles and Peter Selz (eds.) *Theories and Documents of Contemporary Art, A Sourcebook of Artists' Writings* (University of California Press, 1996). The full text was also published on the Arnolfini Gallery's blog on the occasion of Ukeles' one-person international touring exhibition, *Mierle Laderman Ukeles, Maintenance Art Works 1969-1980*, Bristol, September-November 2013. She wrote a second manifesto, a 'Sanitation Manifesto' (1984), also reproduced in Kristine Stiles and Peter Selz (eds.) *Theories and Documents of Contemporary Art* (1996).

3. **Agnes Denes - A Manifesto (1969)**
Copyright © 1969 Agnes Denes. Source: Agnes Denes website. Courtesy, Leslie
Tonkonow Artworks + Projects, New York. This manifesto was incorporated into
a later permanent site-specific commission by the artist, *Poetry Walk - Reflections -
Pools of Thought* (2000), where it is etched on a polished coloured granite slab (c. 4ft x
5 ft), laid in the grounds of University of Virginia, Charlottesville, USA. The 34 other
slabs in the work contain quotes from different poets and philosophers in different
colours and with chopped edges to echo ancient excavations. The artist included
her own manifesto because it 'announced my commitment to a new art form whose
ideals served others, not the self'. (Artist's website). In 2007, it was reproduced in
Hyperion, vol. 2, issue 1, in a special issue of on the artist's work. In 2019, the artist
created a 6-foot scroll of the manifesto as an artist edition of 1,000 copies (designed
by Zak Group) and offered as a gift to students at the Harvard Design School, as her
contribution to the Rouse Visiting Artist Program. In spite of many projects and
major exhibitions worldwide, her first major retrospective in New York, *Agnes Denes:
Absolutes and Intermediates,* took place in 2019 at The Shed, where her manifesto was
reproduced at the entrance to the exhibition.

4. **Michele Wallace - The Manifesto of WSABAL: Women Students and Artists for
    Black Art Liberation: A Student Organization of Black Art Workers (1970)**
Copyright © Michele Wallace. WSABAL was the work of artist Faith Ringgold and her
daughter, the writer Michele Wallace. By way of introduction, Michele Wallace sent
the following statement about WSABAL for the 2014 ebook by KT press: 'In 1970,
Faith Ringgold, my mom and I decided that we needed to found an organization to
represent the interests of black feminist artists. Although we were self-identified black
feminists, we didn't know many other black women who were. So we founded Women
Students and Artists for Black Art Liberation (WSABAL) to cast the umbrella as
wide as possible to draw people, male, female, black and white, into our protests and
various civil disobedience actions to speak truth to power to the art establishment.
The manifesto was composed of the principles of our faith at the time. I wrote the
entire text. I was 18 and very radical, or so I thought. My thinking on these and other
matters has changed considerably since then as can be observed via *Invisibility Blues*
(Verso 1990; 2007); *Dark Designs and Visual Culture* (Duke University Press 2004)
and *Black Macho and The Myth of The Superwoman* (The Dial Press 1979; Verso 1990;
new edition, 2015).'

5. **Nancy Spero - Feminist Manifesto (c. 1970-1971)**
Reproduced in Roel Arkesteijn (ed.) *Codex Spero: Nancy Spero: selected writings and
interviews 1950-2008* (Amsterdam: Roma Publications, 2008) pp.52-53. Reproduced,
courtesy and copyright © Nancy Spero Estate. See also: Jacqueline Skiles and Janet
McDevitt (ed) *A Documentary Herstory of Women Artists in Revolution* (New York:
Women Artists in Revolution, 1971), as Spero played an active part in W.A.R.

6. **Monica Sjöö and Anne Berg - Images on WOMANPOWER - Arts Manifesto (1971)**
Reproduced with permission of Anne Berg and the estate of Monica Sjöö. Copyright
© Anne Berg and Monica Sjöö Estate. Reprinted from *n.paradoxa: international*

feminist art journal vol. 28 (July 2011) pp.64-67. This manifesto was written when the group WOMANPOWER formed in 1971 and was first published in *Towards a Revolutionary Feminist Art* (Bristol, 1972). Monica Sjöö published several editions of this publication in 1971-1972 as a low-cost stapled magazine and in 1974 as 'Some Thoughts on Feminist Art'. WOMANPOWER included Liz Moore, Beverley Skinner, Anne Berg, Rosalyn Smythe and Monica Sjöö. They exhibited together in *WOMANPOWER: 5 Women Artists* at Swiss Cottage Library, London in April 1973. A second shorter version appeared in *MAMA! Women Artists Together* (Birmingham, 1977).

7. **Rita Mae Brown - A Manifesto for the Feminist Artist (1972)**
    First published in *The Furies, Lesbian/Feminist Monthly* Vol. 1, issue 5 (June-July 1972). *The Furies* is archived online at http://www.lesbianpoetryarchive.org/node/131. Used by permission of Brandt & Hochman Literary Agents, Inc. Any electronic copying or distribution of this text is expressly forbidden. All rights reserved. Reproduced courtesy of the author. Copyright © Rita Mae Brown.

8. **VALIE EXPORT - Woman's Art: A Manifesto for the exhibition *MAGNA* (1972)**
    This manifesto was written in March 1972 and first published in *Neues Forum* 228 (Jan 1973) p. 47. Translated from German to English by Regina Haslinger. It was written as a manifesto for the exhibition: *Magna, Feminismus: Kunst und Kreativitat* (Wien/ Vienna, Galerie Nachst St Stephan, 1975), curated by EXPORT, but was not included in the catalogue. It was republished in Kristine Stiles and Peter Selz (eds.) *Theories and Documents of Contemporary Art, A Sourcebook of Artists' Writings* (University of California Press, 1996) and in Helena Reckitt (ed.) *Art and Feminism* (London: Phaidon, 2001) and Will Bradley and Charles Esche (eds) *Art and social change* (London, Afterall, 2007) pp. 202-204. Copyright © Valie Export. Reproduced courtesy of VALIE EXPORT Foundation, Linz.

9. **Carolee Schneemann - Woman in the Year 2000 (1974)**
    This piece was first published in Maggie Tripp (ed) *Woman in the Year 2000* (New York: Arbor House, 1974) pp. 126-128, reprinted in Carolee Schneemann's book *Cezanne, She Was a Great Painter*, (1975) and in German in the catalogue for *Magna, Feminismus: Kunst und Kreativitat* (Wien/ Vienna, Galerie Nachst St Stephan, 1975), p.12, curated by VALIE EXPORT. It was published in English in Carolee Schneemann *More than Meat Joy. Complete Performance Works and Selected writings* (ed.) Bruce McPherson (New Paltz, New York: Documentext, 1979) pp.198-199. It is also reproduced (dated 1977) in Kristine Stiles and Peter Selz (eds.) *Theories and Documents of Contemporary Art, A Sourcebook of Artists' Writings* (University of California Press, 1996) and in Carolee Schneemann *Carolee Schneemann: Imaging her Erotics: Essays, Interviews, Projects* (MIT, 2002). Copyright © Carolee Schneemann Foundation.

10. **Feminist Film and Video Organizations - An On-going Womanifesto (1975)**
    First published in an article by Barbara Halpern Martineau 'Paris: Chicago, Women's Film Festivals,1974' *Women & Film*, 2: 7 (1975) p.11; 'Media Report to Women' (1975) and in Scott MacKenzie (ed.) *Film Manifestos and Global Cinema Cultures: A Critical Anthology* (University of California Press, 2014). Cited in full in Martha Allen

The Development of Communication Networks Among Women, 1963-1983: a history of women's media in the US (Women's Institute for Freedom of the Press, 1988). The manifesto is mentioned in B. Ruby Rich's article, 'The crisis of naming in feminist film criticism' *Jump Cut*, no 19, (December 1978) and in her book *Chick Flicks*, (Duke University Press, 1998) p.73. Reproduced by kind permission of Ariel Dougherty, an organiser of the original conference in 1975. Other organisers were Carol Clement, Phyllis Gomperts and Ann Volkes. Barbara Halpern Martineau (aka Sara Halprin) wielded the pen during the collective drafting of the Womanifesto. Laurel Siebert co-ordinated the conference effort. As Ariel Dougherty indicated in an email, 'We used the word "On-going" at the time with the expectation --dash-- hope that we would build on it over time....The Womanifesto came later'.

11. **Klonaris and Thomadaki - Manifesto for a Radical Femininity for An Other Cinema(1977)**
Copyright © Maria Klonaris/Katerina Thomadaki, Octobre 1977. All rights reserved. First published in *CinémAction I, Dix ans après mai 68, Aspects du cinéma de contestation* (Paris, 1978). The original version of this manifesto is in French on Maria Klonaris/Katerina Thomadaki's website. Translated by Cécile Chich, in collaboration with Katerina Thomadaki. Reproduced, courtesy of Katerina Thomadaki.

12. **Kate Walker - 'Art MANifest versus Arts Feministo' (1977)**
First published in *MAMA! Women Artists Together* (Birmingham, 1977) pp. 22-23. Reproduced courtesy of and © Artist's estate. In this manifesto underlining and graphic marks emphasise the argument e.g.∴= therefore. *MAMA!* reflects on feminist activities in the 1970s including the *Exhibition on Womanpower* at Swiss Cottage Library (1971) (Sjöö and Berg), *A Woman's Place* at 14 Radnor Terrace (1974), *Portrait of the Artist as Housewife* (ICA, 1977), *Feministo* as a postal art event (1975-1976), Women's Workshop, Artists' Union and *Sweet Sixteen and Never Been Shown* (IB King Henry Road, 1975) organised by Women's Free Arts Alliance. The authors include Monica Sjöö, Kate Walker, Anne Berg, Phil Goddall, Liz Moore, Beverley Skinner amongst others.

13. **Z.Budapest, U. Rosenbach, S.B.A. Coven - First Manifesto on the Cultural Revolution of Women (1978)**
Translated from German by Aileen Derieg for the 2014 book by KT press. Reprinted with kind permission of © Ulrike Rosenbach. This manifesto was written while Ulrike Rosenbach was running Schule fur Kreativen Feminismus in Cologne, Germany. See Ulrike Rosenbach 'Schule fur Kreativen Feminismus in Köln (1976-1982)' *n.paradoxa: international feminist art journal* vol. 26 (July 2010) pp. 66-69.

14. **Ewa Partum - Change, My Problem is a Problem of a Woman (1979)**
Copyright © Ewa Partum, Warsaw 1979. The performance/action, *Change, My Problem is a Problem of a Woman*, took place in Galeria Art Forum (Łódź) in 1979. In the performance, the artist talked to the public about cosmetic surgery, about woman as sexual object in patriarchal culture, and about socially conditioned stereotypical images of both men and women. She also presented texts on feminism in art by Lucy Lippard and VALIE EXPORT as recordings played on a tape recorder.

The performance was recorded on film. This event was a different restaging of her 1974 performance of the same name where Partum had half of her face "aged" by professional make-up artists.

15. Women Artists of Pakistan Manifesto (1983)

Reproduced in Salima Hashmi *Unveiling the Visible: Lives and Works of Women Artists of Pakistan* (Pakistan: Sang-e-Meel Publications, 2002). Reproduced courtesy of Salima Hashmi. Although this manifesto was not published at the time of writing, it was written in 1983 at a time of many feminist protests against the military dictatorship of General Mohammad Zia ul-Haq, 1978-1988. The country was under Martial Law. On 12 February 1983, 200 women (lawyers and activists) marched through the streets of Lahore, despite martial law, which prohibited gatherings of more than four people. Their protest was against the law of evidence, which would reduce the testimony of a woman to half that of a man. This manifesto was written against the increasingly oppressive attitude of the State propagated by Zia to maintain power which attempted to promote confining women to *chadar aur char divari* (a veil and four walls). Invisibility, confinement to the home and modesty in dress code are the consequences of this. Several of the signatories were members of the Women's Action Forum (WAF), a mass-based popular front of many women's organisations and concerned individuals, which organised a major petition in 1981 to Zia on women's rights and some of the artists were active organisers, i.e. Lala Rukh and Salima Hashmi. The signatories were prominent artists and writers, Professors and art educators in Pakistan, whose work is today highly celebrated.

16. Chila Kumari Burman - There Have Always Been Great Blackwomen Artists (1986)

This is a synopsis of a talk by Chila Kumari Burman delivered at the Black Visual Artists Forum, ICA, London, 25-26 October 1986. It was first published in *Women Artists Slide Library Journal* No. 15 (February 1987) pp.9-11, then reprinted in Hilary Robinson (ed.) *Visibly Female* (London: Camden Press, 1987). Copyright © Chila Burman. See also: Rina Arya *Chila Kumari Burman: Shakti, Sexuality and Bindi Girls* (KT press, 2012).

17. Gisela Breitling - Feministisches Manifest (1989)

First published in *Feministische Studien*, vol 9, issue s1. https://doi.org/10.1515/fs-1991-s124. English Translation by Sabrina Stolfa for this volume. With the kind permission of Matthias Bonjer, © Estate of Gisela Breitling (1939-2018). www.giselabreitling.de. Gisela Breitling was an artist and art historian, a founder of das Verborgene Museum, Berlin and contributor to many exhibition catalogues, conferences and exhibitions. In 1980, her important book on women in art, *Die Spuren des Schiffs in den Wellen. Eine autobiografische Suche nach den Frauen in der Kunstgeschichte,* was published in Berlin.

18. Riot Grrl Manifesto (1991)

The Riot Grrl Movement began in the early 1990s by Washington State band Bikini Kill and lead singer Kathleen Hanna. The Riot Grrl manifesto was published 1991 in the *BIKINI KILL ZINE 2.* Courtesy of Kathleen Hanna.

19. Eva and Co - The Manifesto (1992)
Copyright © Eva Ursprung, written with Veronika Dreier, Dorothea Konrad, Silvia Ulrich, Anne Wrulich. Translated by Anna Wagner and Kristin Conradi. First published in 1992 when the feminist group, Eva and Co., disbanded. For ten years Eva and Co. had produced a journal, organised exhibitions and projects in Austria and elsewhere and were also a rock band. Reproduced with permission of the authors from http://www.grassrootsfeminism. net/cms/node/243 . Veronika Dreier and Eva Ursprung, with Doris Jauk-Hinz later formed W.A.S. (Womyn's Art Support). See Judith Schwentner 'Kunstverein W.A.S. (Womyn's Art Support) *The Danube Streaming Show*, Veronika Dreier, Doris Jauk-Hinz, Eva Ursprung in conversation with Judith Schwentner' *n.paradoxa: international feminist art journal* vol. 17 (Jan 2006) pp.60-69.

20. VNS MATRIX - Bitch Mutant Manifesto (1994)
Copyright © VNS MATRIX,1994. This text was widely circulated on the net. This version is reproduced from *n.paradoxa online* Issue 4 (August 1997) pp.6-8. VNS Matrix was an artist collective founded in Adelaide, Australia in 1991 by Josephine Starrs, Julianne Pierce, Francesca da Rimini and Virginia Barratt (https://vns.matrix. net). Along with Sadie Plant, the group are credited with the invention of the term "cyberfeminism". One of their earliest projects was *Cyberfeminist Manifesto for the 21st century* (1991), a poster/image/statement smuggled into various websites, placed in the printed advertisements of magazines and posted in public spaces, as well as broadcast over the radio and on television and online in various remix and broadcast forms. See Verena Kuni 'Die Flanerin im Datennetz. Wege und Fragen zum Cyberfeminismus' in Sigrid Schade-Tholen/Georg Christoph Tholen (eds.) *Konfigurationen. Zwischen Kunst und Medien* (Munich, 1999) pp. 467–485 and Louise Mayhew 'VNS Matrix: A case study of women-only collectivism and collaboration in Australia' from her PhD 'Female art collectives and collaborations in Australia c.1970-2010' (University of New South Wales).

21. Xu Hong - Walking out of the Abyss: My Feminist Critique (1994)
Originally published as "Zouchu sheyuan: Wo de nuxingzhuyi piping guan" in *Jiangsu huakan [Jiangsu Pictorial]* vol.163, no.7 (1994). Translated by Lee Ambrozy in Wu Hong (ed) *Contemporary Chinese Art: Primary Documents* (New York, MOMA, 2010). Copyright © Xu Hong. With permission of the author.

22. Violetta Liagatchev - Constitution Intempestive de la Republique Internationale des Artistes Femmes / Untimely Constitution of the International Republic of Female Artists (1995)
Violetta Liagatchev is an artist. This was her contribution to *Masculin-Feminin* (George Pompidou Centre, Paris, 1995-1996). She was born in 1966 in Moscow and has French nationality. She studied at the National Upper School of Fine Art, Paris (1986-1991); Rijksakademie (1992); MA, Marseilles (1993-1994). She has shown her videos, photography, paintings, drawings and artists books in numerous exhibitions in France, Japan and Russia. Copyright © Violetta Liagatchev, November 1995. Reproduced from *n.paradoxa online* Issue 3 (May 1997) pp.44-46. Translated from French by Cécile Chich for KT press.

23. OLD BOYS NETWORK - 100 ANTI-THESES (1997)
Reproduced with permission of Cornelia Sollfrank, © Old Boy's Network.The Old
Boys Network was founded in Berlin in Spring 1997 by Susanne Ackers, Julianne
Pierce, Valentina Djordjevic, Ellen Nonnenmacher and Cornelia Sollfrank. This text
was produced from the first Cyberfeminist International in 1997, a 10-day workshop
with 36 international participants held at Hybrid Workspace, documenta 10, Kassel.
The group's members, publications and activities are documented on their website:
obn.org.

24. LILY BEA MOOR - Lilies of the Valley Unite! Or Not (1998)
Written in Fall 1998, under her pseudonym Lily Bea Moor, this previously
unpublished poem by artist and author Senga Nengudi was first reproduced in the
exhibition catalogue *Double Consciousness: Black Conceptual Art Since 1970* (USA:
Contemporary Arts Museum Houston, 2005), curated by Valerie Cassel Oliver.
Copyright © Senga Nengudi. Courtesy of the artist.

25. Dora García - 100 Impossible Artworks (2001)
Dora García *100 Impossible Artworks* is a text piece by the artist which has been
presented in different formats: as a wall text, as flyers, posters and t-shirts (MUSAC
Collection, León). Copyright © Dora García. Courtesy of the artist.

26. subRosa - Refugia: Manifesto for Becoming Autonomous Zones (BAZ) (2002)
subRosa is a feminist art collective. Current members are Faith Wilding and Hyla
Willis. Courtesy of subRosa. First published in Maria Fernandez, Faith Wilding,
Michelle M. Wright (eds.) *Domain Errors: Cyberfeminist Practices!* (New York:
Autonomedia, 2002). See subRosa 'Bodies Unlimited A decade of subRosa's art
practice' *n.paradoxa: international feminist art journal* vol. 28 (July 2011) pp.16-25.

27. ORLAN - Carnal Art Manifesto / L'Art Charnel (2002)
The Carnal Art Manifesto is reproduced from ORLAN: *Élément Favoris: Exposition
Rétrospective* (Carquefou, France: Frac des Pays de la Loire, 27 Nov. 2002-26 Feb.
2003). It was translated from French by Judith Hayward when it was republished in
n.paradoxa: international feminist art journal vol.12 (July 2003) pp.44-48. Copyright
© ORLAN, courtesy of the artist. It was also published in English in Enright, Robert.
'Beauty and the I of the beholder: a conversation with ORLAN [Out of Actions:
Between Performance & the Object, 1949-1979]' *Border Crossings* (Winnipeg) vol.
17, issue 2, (May 1998) p. 44 and republished in French, by Porte, Mireille Suzanne
Francette. *Inter; Montreal* Vol. 133 (Autumn 2019) p. 9. See also ORLAN *Strip-tease,
Tout sur ma vie, tout sur mon art.* (Editions Gallimard, 2021) p. 135.

28. Rhani Lee Remedes - The S.C.U.B. Manifesto (2002)
Copyright © Rhani Lee Remedes. First published in *LTTR* (2002). Ginger Brooks
Takahashi, K8 Hardy and Emily Roysdon founded *LTTR* in 2001 and this was part of
their inaugural issue in September 2002 titled 'Lesbians to the Rescue'. S.C.U.B. refers
back to Valerie Solanas' *SCUM Manifesto* and mistaken versions of its acronym as
Society for Cutting Up Men.

29. FACTORY OF FOUND CLOTHES - Manifesto (2002)

Copyright © FFC. The Factory of Found Clothes (FFC or Fabrika Nadyonii Odezhdii in Russian, FNO) is Natalya Pershina-Yakimanskaya and Olga Egorova, respectively known as Gluklya and Tsaplya. FFC was founded in 1995 in St Petersburg and has produced works in installation, performance, video, text and 'social research' which develop an operational logic of 'fragility' as subjectivity antagonistic to that which is the state of things – be that the repressive social and political climate of Russia or the reflexive futilities of international art scenes.

30. FEMINIST ART ACTION BRIGADE - Manifesto (2003)

FAAB was formed in Tokyo by the women named as signatories and their collaboration lasted for around one year after the announcement. This text is taken from their announcement of the group on nettime.org (4 Jun 2003) and online at Japan's 'Gender and Arts Project' website. © Reproduced with kind permission of Yoshiko Shimada.

31. Mette Ingvartsen - YES MANIFESTO (2004)

Copyright © Mette Ingvartsen. First published in *Fraktija, Performing Arts Journal.* Reproduced in Astrid Peterle 'The Performances of Mette Ingvartsen: the pleasures of depersonalized bodies, bouncing trampolines and evaporated landscapes' *n.paradoxa: international feminist art journal* vol. 25 (January 2010) p.37 and 'YES MANIFESTO' [metteinvgartsen.net, Accessed 25 October 2009]

32. Manifesto ARCO (2005)

This manifesto was produced at the III International Forum of Contemporary Art Experts, ARCO' 05: 'Cycle 8: Equal opportunity policies in the worlds of art', Madrid, 11th February 2005. THE ROUND TABLES: 'Equal opportunity policies for men and women in the worlds of art: Designing strategies' were organised by Xabier Arakistain, independent curator. Reproduced courtesy of Xabier Arakistain.

33. YES! Association/Föreningen JA! - JämlikhetsAvtal #1 (The Equal Opportunities Agreement #1) (2005) and Equality-Diversity Agreement (2010).

YES! Association/Föreningen JA! (2005-2018) was an art collective, an artwork, an association, an institution, a group of people working to overthrow the ruling system of heteronormative, patriarchal, racist, and capitalist power structures by putting into practice a structural redistribution of access to financial resources, space and time within the art scene. www.foreningenja.org/. YES! Association/Föreningen JA! was founded in 2005 in connection with exhibition *Art Feminism – Strategies and Consequences in Sweden from the 1970s to the Present.* At the exhibition opening, YES! Association/ Föreningen JA! performed Press Conference/ Performance in which they presented gender-specific statistics for the institutions responsible for the exhibition. Towards the end of the press conference, the institutions were invited to sign YES! Association/ Föreningen JA!'s Equal Opportunities Agreement #1. All institutions declined unanimously. Since then, the agreement has been reformulated and renegotiated in relation to different institutions and situations, and now exists in several versions, all aimed at promoting social diversity in the field of art. The activities of YES! Association/Föreningen JA! deal with rights discourse, utopia, assimilation, radical difference, how and if we can name and use identity categories for the purpose of emancipation without reproducing the prevailing discriminatory power structures yet again. As a means to work through these issues YES! Association/ Föreningen JA! uses fiction, enactments and performance. One of the fundamental concepts is to rehearse and/or set in motion a certain situation, and thereby gain experience and skills that can be applied in a future "real-life" situation. Using fiction as a preparation for the future. YES! Association/Föreningen JA! is run by its board co-art workers: Malin Arnell 2005-2018 (founder); Åsa Elzén 2008-2018; Johanna Gustavsson 2005-2011 (founder); Line S. Karlström 2005-2009 (founder); Anna Linder 2005-2007 (founder); Fia-Stina Sandlund 2005-2008 (founder).

34. Arahmaiani - Letter to Marinetti and Manifesto of the Sceptics (2009)
Yogyakarta, July 2009. Copyright © Arahmaiani, Reproduced courtesy of artist. The artist read the 12 articles of 'Manifesto of the Sceptics' at a special performance of the work at the 6th iteration of ACAW's annual forum 'FIELD MEETING: Thinking Collections', premiered offsite in Dubai (Jan 25-26, 2019). In the performance she sat at a desk reading the articles as a defence of what art itself can do as a tool and an alchemical vessel: the combination of rational and moral intelligence and conscience. For her, Art is not an object with just market value but has more importantly human and social values. Projected behind her was her new film, showing the artist at various holy sites in Tibet, the outcome of a long collaboration with Tibetan monks (and local Chinese authorities) to plant 1 million trees across the country. See *Arahmaiani: The Past has not Passed* (Museum Macan, Jakarta, Indonesia: 17 Nov 2018-10 Mar 2019).

35. Elke Krystufek 'Der Sex ist im Text', April 2009
This text was written by Elke Krystufek and used as the press release for her exhibition, *Der Sex ist im Text*, gallery Nicola von Senger, Limmatstrasse 275, 8005 Zürich (19 March - 11 July 2009). Reproduced courtesy of and © the artist, with thanks to Nicola von Senger. Courtesy of Wienerroither & Kohlbacher Gallery. In 2009, Elke Krystufek represented Austria at the Venice Biennale, with *Taboo/Tabou*. The commissioners were VALIE EXPORT and Silvia Eiblmayr.

36. Guerrilla Girls - 'The Guerrilla Girl's Guide to Behaving Badly' (2010)
Copyright © Guerrilla Girls. Reproduced with kind permission of Guerrilla Girls from their website. The Guerrilla Girls, started in 1985, are 'feminist masked avengers in the tradition of anonymous do-gooders like Robin Hood, Wonder Woman and Batman. How do we expose sexism, racism and corruption in politics, art, film and pop culture? With facts, humor and outrageous visuals. We reveal the understory, the subtext, the overlooked, and the downright unfair.' Their work includes the production of posters, t-shirts, artworks, books and speeches protesting sexism and are now the subject of exhibitions. https://www.guerrillagirls.com/

37. Julie Perini - Relational Filmmaking Manifesto (2010)
First published in *INCITE! Journal of Experimental Media* Issue #2, *Radical Aesthetics* (ed.) Brett Kashmere, Fall 2010. Copyright © Julie Perini. Julie Perini borrowed Nicholas Bourriaud's idea of "relational aesthetics" [N. Bourriaud *Relational Aesthetics*

(Paris: les presses du réel, 1998. English translation, 2002)] and adapted it here for a filmmaking practice to explain how her own work addresses traditions of non-fiction filmmaking and video art that are committed to experimentation and destabilisation, and to pursue investigations into liveness and immediacy. See also Perini 'Relational Filmmaking: A Manifesto & Its Explication' in *Afterimage: The Journal of Media Arts and Cultural Criticism* (Rochester, New York) where she discusses the Relational Filmmaking Manifesto in greater detail, with reference to her 2010 video, *Girl Next Door*. Also published in *Afterimage* Vol. 38, Issue 4 (January 2011) pp. 8-10.

38. Elizabeth M. Stephens and Annie M. Sprinkle - ECOSEX MANIFESTO (2011)

Elizabeth M. Stephens and Annie M. Sprinkle's website is Sexecology.org. This is the manifesto for their work linking sex, sexuality and ecology. Copyright © Elizabeth M. Stephens and Annie M. Sprinkle. Annie Sprinkle's one woman show *Post-Porn Modernist* (1989) inspired the 'Post Porn Modernist Manifesto'(1989) written by Veronica Vera for the show's programme.

39. Anetta Mona Chisa and Lucia Tkáčová - 80 : 20 (2011)

Copyright © Anetta Mona Chisa and Lucia Tkáčová. The *80:20* mural was created for the facade of the Romanian Pavilion in Giardini di Castello, Venezia 2011 on the occasion of their participation for Romania. The words were painted in white in two lists on either side of the entrance to the pavilion. The list plays with Pareto's principle or the 80: 20 rule of a vital few (20%) and a trivial many (80%). Pareto had used 80:20 to discuss how 80% of wealth was owned by 20% of people; how 80% of profits were generated by 20% of employees; and 80% of effects produced by 20% causes. In management circles, Pareto's principle also refers to how 20% of effort, time or attention may produce 80% of your results, and why business should prioritise "smart" ways of working in time/effort. As the artists wrote in a statement for the piece: 'the root of the dilemma is an impossible fantasy of escape, of liberation, of stepping out' but 'the system we operate in is not an outer enemy, it is inside of us. We can't get out of it, there's no "outside".'

40. Linda Mary Montano - Money is Green Too Manifesto (2011)

First published in *n.paradoxa: international feminist art journal* Vol. 35. (Jan 2015). Copyright © Linda Mary Montano. Courtesy of artist.

41. Lenka Clayton - An Artist Residency in Motherhood Manifesto (2012)

Copyright © Lenka Clayton. Reproduced with kind permission from her website, www.artistresidencyinmotherhood.com. The Artist Residency in Motherhood she started has been developed internationally through a D.I.Y. kit with 1,200 artists in all 50 US states and 72 countries. As the website suggests, 'You don't have to apply. It doesn't cost anything, it's fully customisable, and you can be in residence for as long as you choose. You don't even have to travel, the residency takes place entirely inside your own home and everyday life.' The project began with this manifesto, business cards, a site to explore (motherhood), mentors, improvements to her studio, materials, and three mornings a week childcare for her newborn son in Pittsburgh, Pennsylvania. Clayton now runs an extensive mentoring programme.

42. **Silvia Ziranek - MANIFESTA (2013)**
Copyright © scz. An early version of this previously unpublished manifesto was printed by Crescent Arts, Scarborough, for The Art Party, November 2013. See also Silvia Ziranek *Wall Works: Selected Writings and Performances* (KT press ebook, 2013). As the author wrote in an email about the text: 'QUALITY = EQUALITY. I TRY BREVITY. I WRITE (I HOPE) WITH PASSION, SUCCINCT NOT SENTIMENTAL. I URGE: I'M STILL URGENT AFTER ALL THESE Y/EARS. ART MUST BE PART OF. ART IS PART, NOT AP/ART. "TOO CLEVER BY HALF" IS THE ENGLISH ADAGE; SHAME ON YOU, SHIRKING CHALLENGE.'

43. **Alexandra Pirici and Raluca Voinea - 'Manifesto for the Gynecene - Sketch of a New Geological Era' (2015)**
First published in Stephan Geene, Gesine Strempel und Jennifer Sophia Theodor (eds) *dea ex machina* (Germany: Merve Books, 2015) and *Paletten* (Sweden) vol. 300, Issue 2 (2015) pp. 4-8. This manifesto was quickly translated into several European languages and widely circulated. In the manifesto, they position 'the feminine as equivalent not to a gender but to a condition, not a "natural" condition but a cultural one. The feminine is the first stage towards a transgressive humanism and the Gynecene is the first global and simultaneous transfer of the feminine imprint onto the physical and political strata (deeply connected as they are today) of the Earth.' Through this condition, they aim to redefine politics, technology, ecology and care, as well as feminism. Copyright and with permission of authors.

44. **Representatives of Prague Art Institutions - 'Feminist (Art) Institution: Code of practice' (2017).**
This Code of Practice for a feminist art institution is one of the outputs of a seminar held in spring as part of the tranzit.cz 2017 programme. The seminar examined the possible forms of organisations and collectives that wish to be seen as feminist. The organisers thank Ewa Majewska, Xabier Arakistain, Giovanna Zapperi and Luba Kobová who spoke at these events.

45. **n i i c h e g o d e l a t - Research Institute for Doing Nothing (2017-2021)**
This previously unpublished manifesto was authored in St Petersburg by: Nadezhda Ishkinyaeva, Katya Ivanova, Anna Averyanova, Marina Shamova, Yozhi Stolet, Alexandra Abakshina, Marina Russkikh, Marya Dmitrieva, Marina Israilova, Masha Ivasenko, Ilya Firdman, Sin Out, Suzanna Oriordan, Natalia Rybalko. Translated to English by collective labor, © artists. The group partially inherits the cyberfeminist approaches of the Cyberfeminist Club in St. Petersburg in the 1990s and some art-activists who graduated from School of Engaged Art organised by Chto Delat. The group has been active organising lectures, festivals, events and conducting different art researches, theatre performances researching imagination of bio technology, male pregnancy (Aleksandra Abakshina) for 4 years. They produced a play «44 Versions of Future» published in *Teatp* (St Petersburg) №44, 2021. Their work is available on YouTube and at https://www.facebook.com/niichegodelat/

46. **Gluklya / Natalia Pershina-Yakimanskaya -'Manifesto of the Utopian Union of Unemployed People' (2017)**
This text was developed for the performative demonstration *Carnival of the Oppressed Feelings* in Amsterdam, October 28 2017 and edited by Theo Tegelaers. Copyright © Gluklya, reproduced with permission of the artist. http://gluklya.com/

47. **We are Not Surprised (WANS) - 'We are Not Surprised' (2017)**
Open Letter reproduced as Creative Commons. The letter was released online, widely reported on, and reprinted in art journals around the world. We are Not Surprised is the art world's #MeToo moment. It was triggered by events reported on 24 October by *artnet News* about accusations of sexual harassment and sexual misconduct by Knight Landesman, co-publisher of *Artforum*, who stepped back from board membership (but not share ownership) in an attempt to close down accusations against him. Amanda Schmitt, a former intern and employee (2009-2012), brought charges against Landesman and the magazine for retaliation and sexual harassment. Other women who came forward with similar complaints did not proceed to the courts.
This open letter 'began as discussion between eight Instagram members before it was moved to the more secure WhatsApp and the team communication app Slack' (Jennifer Thatcher, 'No Surprises' *Art Monthly* 414, March 2018)). Minor editorial changes were made until 11 p.m. on October 29 2017, EST. The online letter was quickly signed by 3,000 women and reportedly signed by 9,500 people by midnight on 30 October 2017. As the international response to the letter made clear, the abuse and misuse of power of those with authority or as employers which leads to women's harassment and sexual exploitation in the workforce remaining unchecked and with few consequences is not confined to this one case. The group had a London as well as New York branch and ran a website and social media groups with *ad hoc* meetings for several years. The title of the group is a reference to one of Jenny Holzer's *Truisms*: 'Abuse of power comes as no surprise.' Amanda Schmidt received damages in 2021 from Artforum for retaliation against her because she complained, but her case against Landesman did not proceed because of the 5 year statutory time limit on making a complaint.

48. **Nosotras Propemos / Permanent Assembly of Women Art Workers - 'We propose: Declaration of Commitment to Feminist Practices in Art' (2017)**
This statement was written in Spanish and quickly translated into English, French, Italian, Portuguese and German. By midnight on November 24 2017, 2,742 people had signed it. English translation by Jane Brodie from https://nosotrasproponemos.org/. The impetus for this proposal was the unexpected and premature death of Argentine artist Graciela Sacco, which brought together a group of women artists to discuss what could be done, not only in her memory, but also for changing the situation of women artists. On November 7, 2017, the group founded the Permanent Assembly of Art Workers, known as Nosotras Propemos, to promote feminist practices, to call on the global art community and to organise the International Women's Strike on March 8, 2018. In 2019 and 2020, Nosotras Propemos joined other women activists on the streets with actions for International Women's Day. Many different interventions have been organised by the group: including a call for better representation of women artists in Argentina's national

salon prizes in 2018; "Rescuing Other Narratives", an intervention in Buenos Aires' Museums Nights to "rescue" work by "forgotten" female artists from their collections, encouraging museums to turn off the lights on male artists and instead spotlight works by women; organising exhibitions by Juana Lumerman (1905-1982) at National Museum of Fine Arts; Ana Maria Moncalvo (1921-2009) at the Sivori Museum, and Mara Facchin (1962-2018) at the Buenos Aires, Museum of Modern Art. The group also organised many workshops and meetings for women artists to discuss equality and solidarity. Reproduced with kind permission of group and Andrea Giunta.

49. **Feminist Art and Architecture Collaborative (FAAC) - To Manifest**
This manifesto was the product of the workshop "FAAC Your Syllabus!" (April 21-22, 2018), convened by the Feminist Art and Architecture Collaborative (FAAC). During the two-day workshop 18 international feminist educators, activists, and curators met, discussed the feminisms that influenced them (textual or otherwise), debated pedagogical methodologies and their syllabi on art, architecture, and visual and cultural studies. Convening members were Ana María León, Andrea J. Merrett, Armaghan Ziaee, Catalina Mejía Moreno, Charlotte Kent, Elaine Stiles, Emma Cheatle, Jennifer Chuong, Juliana Maxim, Katherine Guinness, Louisa Iarocci, Martina Tanga,Olga Touloumi, Rebecca Choi, Susanō Surface, Saher Sohail, Sarah Parrish, Tessa Paneth-Pollak. The session was funded by the Global Architectural History Teaching Collaborative and hosted by Columbia University. It aligned with *Now What?! Advocacy, Activism, and Alliances in American Architecture since 1968*, a travelling exhibition by ArchiteXX which opened at the Siegel Gallery, Pratt University, New York, 2018. This text was first published in *Harvard Design Magazine*, No 46, *No Sweat*, 2018, © authors. Original design by Jiminie Ha/With Projects Inc.. Feminist Art and Architecture Collaborative (FAAC) is a transnational and intersectional feminist research group that labors in the production of new pedagogies for art and architecture disciplines. https://faacweb.wordpress.com/

50. **MANIFIESTO NO, NEIN, NIET !!!!! (2018)**
Published in Spanish in Bilbao, 15th November 2018, following Xavier Arakistain's speech about this manifesto and ARCO 2005 at the Conference on Art, Research and Feminisms, 14th-15th November 2018, Bizkaia Aretoa UPV/EHU (University of the Basque Country). Translated into English by Jessica Adler for this book. The book, edited by Andrea Abalia Marijuan / Txaro Arrazola-Oñate Tojal, *Arte, Investigación y Feminismos* (UPV/EHU, 2020) was another outcome of the event. In 2008, Xavier Arakistain, then Director of Centro Cultural Montehermoso Kulturunea, Vitoria-Gasteiz (2007 to 2011), with feminist anthropologist Lourdes Méndez, started to organise a yearly interdisciplinary, international and intergenerational course, *Artistic Production and the Feminist Theory of Art: New Debates*. Between 2012 and 2018, the course took place at Azkuna Zentroa, Bilbao, and since 2019 as *The Feminist Gaze. Feminist Perspectives in Art Production and Theories of Art* the course is held at the Museo de Arte Contemporáneo del País Vasco, ARTIUM.

No Manifesto (1965) - A Manifesto Reconsidered (2008)

Yvonne Rainer

(1965)	(2008)
no to spectacle	avoid if at all possible.
no to virtuosity	acceptable in limited quantity.
no to transformations and magic and make-believe	magic is out; the other two are sometimes tolerable.
no to the glamour and transcendence of the star image	acceptable only as quotation.
no to the heroic	dancers are ipso facto heroic.
no to the anti-heroic	don't agree with that one.
no to trash imagery	don't understand that one.
no to involvement of performer or spectator	spectators: stay in your seats.
no to style	style is unavoidable.
no to camp	a little goes a long way.
no to seduction of spectator by the wiles of the performer	unavoidable.
no to eccentricity	if you mean "unpredictable," that's the name of the game.
no to moving or being moved	unavoidable.

MANIFESTO!

MAINTENANCE   ART   --   Proposal   for   an   exhibition
"CARE"
© 1969

Mierle Laderman Ukeles

I. IDEAS:

    A. The Death Instinct and the Life Instinct:

        The Death Instinct: separation, individuality, Avant-Garde
par excellence; to follow one's own path to death -- do your
own thing, dynamic change.

        The Life Instinct: unification, the eternal return, the
perpetuation and MAINTENANCE of the species, survival
systems and operations, equilibrium.

    B. Two basic systems: Development and Maintenance. The sourball
           of every revolution: after the revolution, who's
           going to pick up the garbage on Monday morning?
Development: pure individual creation; the new; change;
           progress, advance, excitement, flight or fleeing.
Maintenance: keep the dust off the pure individual
           creation; preserve the new; sustain the change;
           protect progress; defend and prolong the
           advance;renew the excitement; repeat the flight;

              show your work -- show it again
              keep the contemporaryartmuseum groovy
              keep the home fires burning

Development systems are partial feedback systems with major
        room for change.
Maintenance systems are direct feedback systems with little
        room for alteration.

C.   Maintenance is a drag; it takes all the fucking time(lit.)
            The mind boggles and chafes at the boredom. The
            culture confers lousy status on maintenance
            jobs = minimum wages, housewives = no pay.

      clean your desk, wash the dishes, clean the floor,
      wash your clothes, wash your toes, change the baby's
      diaper, finish the report, correct the typos, mend
      the fence, keep the customer happy, throw out the
      stinking garbage, watch out don't put things in your
      nose, what shall I wear, I have no sox, pay your bills,
      don't litter, save string, wash your hair, change the
      sheets, go to the store, I'm out of perfume, say it
      again -- he doesn't understand, seal it again -- it
      leaks, go to work, this art is dusty, clear the table,
      call him again, flush the toilet, stay young.

D.   Art:

      Everything I say is Art is Art. Everything I do is Art
      is Art. "We have no Art, we try to do everything
      well." (Balinese saying).

   Avant-garde art, which claims utter development, is infected
      by strains of maintenance ideas, maintenance activities,
      and maintenance materials.
            -- Process art especially claims pure development
               and change, yet employs almost purely
               maintenance processes.

E.   The exhibition of Maintenance Art, "CARE", would zero
      in on pure maintenance, exhibit it as contemporary art,
      and yield, by utter opposition, clarity of issues.

II. THE MAINTENANCE ART EXHIBITION: Three parts: personal,general,
     and Earth Maintenance.

   A.   Personal Part:

              I am an artist. I am a woman. I am a wife. I am
                   a mother (random order).
              I do a hell of a lot of washing, cleaning, cooking,
                   renewing, supporting, preserving, etc. Also,
                   (up to now separately) I "do" Art.
         Now, I will simply do these maintenance everyday things,
         and flush them up to consciousness, exhibit them, as Art.
         I will live in the museum as I customarily do at home
         with my husband and my baby, (right, or if you don't
         want me around at night I would come in every day)
         for the duration of the exhibition and do all these
         things as public Art activities: I will sweep and wax
         the floors, dust everything, wash the walls (i.e. "floor
         paintings, dust works, soap-sculpture, wall-paintings"),
         cook, invite people to eat, clean up, put away, change
         light bulbs. I might save and make agglomerations and
         dispositions of all functional refuse. The exhibition
         area might look "empty" of art, but it will be maintained
         in full public view.

         My working will be the work.

   B.   General Part: Everyone does a hell of a lot of noodiling
        maintenance work. The general part of the exhibition
        would consist of interviews of two kinds.

        1.   Previous individual interviews of, say, 50 different
               classes and kinds of occupations that run a
               gamut from "maintenance man", maid, sanitation
               man, mailman, union man, construction worker,
               librarian, grocerystore man, nurse, doctor,
               teacher, museum director, salesman, baseball
               player, child, criminal, bank president, mayor,
               movie star, artist, etc., about: what they think
               maintenance is; how they feel about spending
               whatever parts of their lives on maintenance
               activities; what is the relationship between
               maintenance and freedom; what is the relationship
               between maintenance and life's dreams.

               These interviews will be typed and exhibited.

2

2. Interview Room--for spectators at the Exhibition:
    A room of desks and chairs where professional (?)
    interviewers will interview the spectators at the
    exhibition along same questions as typed interviews
    (in 1, above). The responses should be personal.

    These interviews are taped and replayed throughout
    the exhibition area.

C. Earth Maintenance:

Everyday, a container of the following kinds of refuse
will be delivered to the Museum: 1) the contents of
one sanitation truck; 2) a container of polluted air;
3) a container of polluted Hudson River; 4) a container
of ravaged land. Once at the exhibition, each container
will be serviced: purified, de-polluted, rehabilitated,
recycled, and conserved by various technical (and / or
pseudo-technical) procedures either by myself or
scientists.

These servicing procedures are repeated for the duration
of the exhibition.

A MANIFESTO (1969)

AGNES DENES

WORKING WITH A PARADOX
DEFINING THE ELUSIVE
VISUALIZING THE INVISIBLE
COMMUNICATING THE INCOMMUNICABLE
NOT ACCEPTING THE LIMITATIONS SOCIETY HAS ACCEPTED
SEEING IN NEW WAYS

LIVING FOR A FRACTION OF A SECOND AND PENETRATING
LIGHT YEARS — MEASURING TIME IN THE EXTREME DISTANCES —
LONG BEFORE AND BEYOND LIVING EXISTENCE

USING INTELLECT AND INSTINCT TO ACHIEVE INTUITION

STRIVING TO SURPASS HUMAN LIMITATIONS BY SEARCHING
THE MYSTERIES AND PROBING THE SILENT UNIVERSE, ALIVE
WITH HIDDEN CREATIVITY

ACHIEVING TOTAL SELF-CONSCIOUSNESS AND SELF-
AWARENESS

PROBING TO LOCATE THE CENTER OF THINGS — THE TRUE
INNER CORE OF INHERENT BUT NOT YET UNDERSTOOD
MEANING — AND EXPOSE IT TO BE ANALYZED

BEING CREATIVELY OBSESSIVE

QUESTIONING, REASONING, ANALYZING, DISSECTING AND
RE-EXAMINING

UNDERSTANDING THAT EVERYTHING HAS FURTHER MEANING,
THAT ORDER HAS BEEN CREATED OUT OF CHAOS,
BUT ORDER, WHEN IT REACHES A CERTAIN TOTALITY
MUST BE SHATTERED BY NEW DISORDER

AND BY NEW INQUIRIES AND DEVELOPMENTS

FINDING NEW CONCEPTS, RECOGNIZING NEW PATTERNS

UNDERSTANDING THE FINITUDE OF HUMAN EXISTENCE
AND STILL STRIVING TO CREATE BEAUTY AND PROVOCATIVE
REASONING

RECOGNIZING AND INTERPRETING THE RELATIONSHIP OF
CREATIVE ELEMENTS TO EACH OTHER: PEOPLE TO PEOPLE,
PEOPLE TO GOD, PEOPLE TO NATURE, NATURE TO NATURE,
THOUGHT TO THOUGHT, ART TO ART

SEEING REALITY AND STILL BEING ABLE TO DREAM

DESIRING TO KNOW THE IMPORTANCE OR INSIGNIFICANCE
OF EXISTENCE

PERSISTING IN THE ETERNAL SEARCH

THE MANIFESTO OF WSABAL
WOMEN STUDENTS AND ARTISTS FOR BLACK ART LIBERATION
A STUDENT ORGANIZATION OF BLACK ART WORKERS (1970)

THE FUNCTIONS OF WSABAL:-

To inform the Student Public of the Esthetic Oppression of Black Women in the Visual Arts

This Esthetic Oppression Comes in the Forms of:

Brown Art shows filled with Token Art Niggas which are being passed off for Black Art Shows.

Anti-Human Art Shows which are being passed off for Protest Shows.

The exclusion of Black Women Artists from ALL shows because of their position as the only generation which is creating A Revolution in Art.

To Encourage All Students to Protest and Challenge All Trends Against Art for People

WSABAL has done this most recently in the cases of:

Letters to the *New York Times* in response to articles written by Hilton Kramer, "Uncle" Benny Andrews and Edmund Gaither concerning the show - Afro-American Artists: New York & Boston - which intentionally excluded black women for the purpose of leading the public to believe that the BROWN SHIT ART done by black male artists was Black Art; and for the purpose of projecting particular Token Art Niggas which do not threaten the Anti-Human Art establishment.

A commitment which was expressed in a letter to Edmund Gaither, the organizer of the Boston Brown Shit Art Show to actively oppose all Brown Art Shows which are meant to oppress all real art in the future.

A demonstration against the Venice Biennale Show at the School of Visual Arts on July 6th at 3:30 p.m. because of its exclusion of women, blacks and black women; and because of its intention to disguise the exhibition as a protest show when it was actually another implementation of Anti-Human Art and a projection of superstars.
It appears, at least for the moment, that THE EMERGENCY CULTURAL GOVERNMENT COMMITTEE has complied to WSABAL's first demand by making the Venice Biennale Show open.

Notice of this change was not in the papers, nor have we seen it written anywhere. WSABAL suspects that the arrangement will be the following: The Anti-Human artists will be exhibited in the Gallery, and the black artists and women artists will be exhibited in the lobby. If this be the case, WSABAL will protest this segregation. WSABAL demands that the art works be totally integrated throughout the lobby and the gallery. WSABAL invites all students to see that the superstars projection of these Anti-Human Artists be stopped.

To Support the Exposure of Real Black Art Which is Done by Black Women Who, As Mothers and Sisters, Are Concerned With the Afro-American Situation of Today

We supply the black women with a liberated voice to protest bigotry on the part of black and white male artists against black women artists.

We are destroying the walls that separate the art of black women from the view of the people by exposing so called black art shows as Brown Shit Art Shows, and so called protest shows as Anti-Human Art Superstar shows.

We are revitalizing an interest in black art among students, outraged by social injustices, and thus we are bringing an end to the disenchantment of ALL students with ALL art.

WSABAL's DEFINITION OF BLACK ART

Black Art is Truth Which Is -

The Black Color of our skin.

Rhythm which is the major black artistic contribution.

An artistic heritage which comes from the Principles of African Art.

The severity of our oppression, our persistent will to survive, and our determination to effect a liberated society.

Black Art is Not:

All Brown Shit (or all male).

"Picture" art.

Political propaganda or prediction of The Future.

Black Art Talk (we don't talk it, we do it).

Token Nigga Art.

Mainstream copy whitey art.

THE MAJOR DEMAND OF WSABAL

ALL GROUP SHOWS ARE TO BE OPENED TO THE PARTICIPATION OF ALL ART WORKERS THROUGHOUT AMERICA

All shows are to be fifty percent women.

All shows which are not a stated projection of a particular cultural group, such as Afro-American, American Indians, American Whites, etc., must reflect the ethnic distribution of the metropolitan area in which the show is being given.

WSABAL'S PRIMARY INTEREST IS IN THE OPPRESSION OF BLACK WOMEN ARTISTS

By Michele Wallace - Art Writer
WSABAL,
Harlem,
New York.

FEMINIST MANIFESTO (c. 1970-1971)

NANCY SPERO

> "...male/female relationships are essentially asymmetrical;
> men dominate women, at least jurally, in all human societies"
> Harold W. Scheffler *Structuralism in Anthropology*

> "Papa's little bed pal. Lump of love."
> James Joyce *Ulysses*

The arts, like all areas of activity, are pre-empted by men. It is male territory governed by the tacit "laws" of male supremacy. Art is always viewed in the aggressive histories of male dominance. As viewed by the male ego, art is masculine. There is no feminine counterpart (even when the arts are considered effete, it is in terms of male effeteness rather than thru so-called over-femininized attributes of delicacy and restraint even if such attributes could be given biological verification.

There are many women artists, many who are well-known, but art itself is viewed as masculine and the product of aggressive male instincts imbued with masculine hero-worship and male-style notoriety. The term "avant-garde" referring as it does to military nomenclature is aggressive-militaristic in origin, and avant-garde notions in art are masculinised versions of revolt, clearly contained within a masculinised status quo.

Women artists are supposed to be servile by training and history. In this male bourgeois social order, a woman is as good as a man, only less so — and her art is as good as a man's, only less so — and those women who are celebrated as artists are celebrated, only less so.

Female museum personnel, female gallery owners and female critics in the characterizations and distributions of contemporary art are even more dominated by sexism than female artists. Feminine inclusion in museum collection exhibitions, gallery groups, etc, is well below 10%. A rapid survey of artists represented in the Whitney Museum collection of American art reveals 8% female, 92% male.

The woman artist demands an autonomy equal to man's. Women artists must rebel against the male caste and economic control (male imperialism is based on a primitive "biological" separation of roles). Women artists are increasingly angry and militant.

In the future there may be feminine or masculine arts, but this will appear under the aegis of some more ultimate liberation. Today there is an art that is a mixture of the history of what has been, a diffused asexual generalized art. This would be fine were it not dominated in all its external manifestations by simplistic male-ego drives.

The ultimate liberation of women is the hardest and most ultimate task of revolution because her biological subordination has been so historical and determined. (The ultimate liberation of men from repressive and sexist roles is the equally difficult complimentary male task of revolution). It is so deep-rooted in the so-called rhythms of nature that to break with it is to create a virtually new order of creature co-equal to man. Then art will change. This is the future.

But the future is in the future. Women artists today condemn male dominance in a bourgeois society. We condemn male suprematist elitism. Women artists demand the immediate break-up of the repressive, sexist male ego domination of museums, galleries, etc. We demand that equality of movement and opportunity taken for granted by men. We demand a new kind of space, a space free from repression to develop the roles of freedom.

IMAGES ON WOMANPOWER - ARTS MANIFESTO (1971)
(trying to give a rough and necessarily incomplete idea of
what we are about)

MONICA SJÖÖ and ANNE BERG

We are the artists of the oppressed peoples.

We as women bear on our shoulders oppression stretching back
into the ancient past.

---- WE WERE THE FIRST OPPRESSED ----

We reject the abstract researches, playful gimmicks characteristic
of contented and successful solo artists. Although aware that these
pursuits are not entirely without purpose and interest, we feel
that it is NOT possible as members of an oppressed group - half of
the human race - and with powerful means of communication in our
hands to sit around playing games with the surface of reality.

We accept that early 20th century artists had to escape from
Victorian romantic illusions and embrace reality (beyond illusion)
via cubism and collage. Like scientists they were trying to get at
the reality of vision on the level of atoms and cell-structures,
the light and forms that make up what we consider to be the everyday
world. In the early 20th century painters were enthusiastic about
technology because it seemed to hold the seeds of the future.
Futurism, constructivism sought to explore technological reality
- but NOW technology is emerged in a commercialism so obscene and
decadent that for artists to embrace such values is beyond our
comprehension.

Commercial life is the enemy of art and art cannot accept its
visual signs as part of our language. DEATH TO THE PLASTIC CULTURE.
Our century has tried to make art a part of reality, but the reality
in our culture is crass, exploitative, capitalistic reality and our
function as artists should be to expose the sickness of this culture
and NOT to embrace it.

Perhaps the only thing that can serve us now is sort of tragic
realism which is not expressionism because it is too real.

Nature and Machine cannot live together - the living tissue is
ground to dust... "A small and beautiful child walks thru the blasted
scene of disaster - a scene that is atomized and disintegrated by
the last convulsions of a society that will not die, but hangs on,
desiring to bring everything to dust, amongst violent tombs of
sordidity and despair, supermarkets and bingo halls." Where is the
glorious new world of the machine?

Art, like science, must explore the world, attempt to heal it;

abstract art now serves the ruling classes because it mystifies reality, it is undangerous, undisturbing – it has become like patterns on the level of interior decoration, the tedious technicalities of advertising. It cannot be used as a tool either exploring mystical reality or exploring social reality. WE REJECT IT. WE SAY NO TO EMPTY ABSTRACTIONS, to the 'art for art's sake' philosophy of the privileged white middle-class male artworld. WE THE OPPRESSED cannot afford this empty play with words and forms, for us the import and task is to convey to people to WOMEN – their dignity and strength and beauty – OUR PAST AND FUTURE. God-Woman giving birth to the universe out of her bloody womb, life, death, rebirth – the eternal mystery of life and its richness.

HOW DOES ONE COMMUNICATE WOMEN'S STRENGTH, STRUGGLE, RISING UP FROM OPPRESSION, BLOOD, CHILDBIRTH, SEXUALITY – IN STRIPES AND TRIANGLES, the time is past when women dared not portray their fears, hatred, experience of oppression – we are no longer afraid to show in images the violence of our anger and remorse, and also our great sadness and love.

True life and inspiration know no false limits and prejudice as to technical means.

Almost every male artist in the past was a member of the elite. Their leisure was bought at the cost of mothers, daughters, sisters, wives – who were allowed to be workers, models, supporters, secretaries, drudges but NEVER allowed themselves to create. (as well as reaping the wealth created by the working class and third world peoples)

We, the ones, who have been subjected to humiliation every day of our lives, denied our identity, history and tradition, are not the ones to stand back coolly and analytically take of objectivity and abstraction. So-called objectivity – what is it but the separation of thought and reason from our real desires and wishes? Men use the terms to hide they have desires and wishes. Women are expected to follow suit and deny their own.

FUCK YOUR "OBJECTIVITY" AND YOUR MIDDLE-CLASS CULTURE.

We want to give expression to the REAL hopes needs and beliefs of women – of people – struggling to escape from oppression both material and psychological – servitude and contempt.

Even our history must be rewritten. Are we to continue bearing the myth that women are, have been, and will be passive, uncreative, and mentally inferior? The split between body-soul, material-spirit is

a false separation of patriarchal civilizations who have formulated
theories and philosophies over thousands of years excusing and
re-inforcing our oppression by saying that women represent the
negative, the dark, the passive, the non-creative and non-spiritual
aspect and matter that men have to surpass and exploit in order to
become pure spirit, pure activity, pure artist, aggressive – and
defined by men – positive energy.

LIES AND LIES ARE WE BRED ON!
We are slaves with the consciousness of slaves.
But myths are not destroyed solely by social change and logic.

Women painters wish to destroy the myth of inferiority and
replace it with a new pride and joy in womanhood – in sisterhood –
and of all aspects of life that have been deformed and brutalized
by capitalism and the patriarchal atomized family. We also want to
release men from their narrow pseudo-scientific dogmatism, the need
to assert and subjugate in order to feel strong (some men cannot
get a 'hard-on' unless they degrade and humiliate a woman sexually
and mentally). Womankind, like the surface of this earth, has been
ravaged because of this false need.

But now WE ARE RISING to re-recreate at last our strength,
dignity, wisdom, and creativity of woman of the ancient past.

WE WISH TO ACHIEVE A WORLD VIEW.

In ancient cultures life and art were integrated. Art was the
great religious rituals – the initiation dramas that expressed the
collective dreams and experience of the whole community concerning
life and the universe. Music, dance, masks, carvings, murals, all
served a purpose and together they created a wholeness. But..art
which had once been the expression of both sexes became later divided
into the Sacred and the Profane. Sacred art became a male province
in the hands of a male priesthood, when the priestesses of the Great
Mother were deposed at the beginning of the patriarchal era, and
women were left with the 'lesser arts' of pottery, weaving, etc.

Our dreams, hopes, feelings, cannot be realized in present
patriarchal, capitalistic society that denies all experience or
expression that does not serve the exploitation of aspirations,
feelings, intuition and experience of women.

WOMEN LIVE A SHADOW LIFE.

There is a one-sex view of art today; what we always see is the
men's vision of himself, the world, and women. We are sick, sick,

sick of the continual visual exploitation of women's bodies, of
women as objects. 'I paint with my prick' said Renoir - only too
true……

But we are women and WE ARE SUBJECTS and will portray ourselves
as such and so at last we will end the ages of pornography - vision
of women. If a woman dares to portay a man as her sexual object
there is outcry heard all over the land. [Editor's note - Monica
Sjoo did just that and her work was ordered to be taken down by
police - in the haven of artists - St. Ives, Cornwall]

We are told we are not in the mainstream of artistic exploration,
that we are not exploring modern forms; that we are 'out on a limb'
- but we tell you that IT IS YOU WHO ARE ON A LIMB!

What you have now is a half-world imagery at the point of
stagnation. Women are presently accepted into the art world only if
they conform to the acceptable attitude of the already dominant male
art view of what art is and was; again HIS vision. Male artists have
explored every aspect of the half world view and expression, they
express frustration in thrusting big, bigger, and biggest objects
and canvasses, all with no content whatsoever and with no relation
to real human feelings or aspirations. They have reached a dead end.

But for women our explorations start now - we do not identify
creative energy with phallic thrusting aggressiveness. Perhaps
women have in fact great artistic traditions in the ancient past.
Who created the cave paintings? If one knows that the cave was a
womb and the sanctuary of the Great Mountain Mother, who was served
by female priests and who was the mother of all animals, one can
well ask if the murals were not the work of women. Pottery was
invented by women and the forms and patterns of ancient pottery are
some of the greatest treasures of the past. The palaces of Crete
with their beautiful murals and central heating systems - were not
they the work of women painters and architects? In Africa women
are musicians and dancers, they have secret songs and dances. Why
so little is known about female cultures is because the majority
of anthropologists have been men and these women's initiations
and secret societies are not open to men observers. In folk music
in England a great many of the recorded folksongs were taken down
from women singers. In America there was a whole tradition of
blues singers like Bessie Smith and Ma Rainey. So little is known
about women's art because male historians have little interest
in recording what women have created and achieved. It has been a
positive embarrassment to them but human life is an inter-action
between two sexes. Art must be the expression of the total human
world and only art fed by female and male views inter-acting can be
vital. The time is NOW and it is overdue!

A MANIFESTO FOR THE FEMINIST ARTIST (1972)

Art in the past has been the pursuit of the privileged with few exceptions, it has been white, male, usually middle to upper class, and overwhelmingly heterosexual. All forms of the arts — music, dance, literature, painting, film, etc. — reflect the concerns of this dominant group with a few male homosexuals thrown in for good measure. Only recently have the concerns of other people and their art begun to emerge, especially within the Black community, and in its beginning stages among women.

Today 90% of what is available to the public remains the art of the oppressor. Since they control the business end of the arts they control what is presented to people. Therefore precious little of our work leaks out to the mass public. But their arts for all its dominance is in such decline it has reached the final stages of disease and decadence. That art offers us two poles: nostalgia and porno-violence. Both come from emptiness, starvation of creativity and hope, and incredible self-indulgence.

Their concept of self has become so perverted that older members of the oppressor generation seek the coordination of their fragmented selves on a graph of the past, nostalgia. Meanwhile the younger generation gives itself in an orgy of porno-violence. The male ego is so eroded that these younger men — the inheritors of the political-economic reins of the death culture — seek an affirmation of self in violent, destructive sex. Porno-violence is their symbol of protest that in its essence denies not only dignity and equality to women but even life to women. Rape is the cliché of male art be it individual rape or the systematic brutalization of an entire sex and entire races.

As women artists we are in deep revolt against this rotting art just as we are in revolt against the syphilitic political structures that damage us and endanger world peace.

Our experiences have been locked away from the eyes and ears of the people. We must fight to transmit those experiences forcing people to face the reality of our lives, of all oppressed people's lives. But our art must be more than personal narrative; it must contain a vision for the future where no group rapes another, where force is not the heart of politics and egotism not the mind of art.

Our task is to achieve a synthesis of poetry and politics, theater and experience, love and society. We have to pull together a world compartmentalized by the resident schizophrenics in the White House, the Pentagon and General Motors. We have to build an alternate media, a new art to help us create a new government in which all people are free. Let our work be the bridge to that new world. RMB.

WOMAN'S ART

A MANIFESTO for the exhibition *MAGNA* (1972)

THE POSITION OF ART IN THE WOMEN'S LIBERATION MOVEMENT
IS THE POSITION OF WOMAN IN THE ART'S MOVEMENT.

THE HISTORY OF WOMAN IS THE HISTORY OF MAN,
  because man has defined the image of woman for both man and woman, men create and control the social and communication media such as science and art, word and image, fashion and architecture, social transportation and division of labor. men have projected their image of woman onto these new media, and in accordance with these medial patterns they gave shape to woman. if reality is a social construction and men its engineers, we are dealing with a male reality. women have not yet come to themselves, because they have not had a chance to speak insofar as they had no access to the media.
  let women speak so that they can find themselves, this is what I ask for in order to achieve a self-defined image of ourselves and thus a different view of the social function of women. we women must participate in the construction of reality via the building stones of media-communication.
  this will not happen spontaneously or without resistance, therefore we must fight! if we shall carry through our goals such as social equal rights, self-determination, a new female consciousness, we must try to express them within the whole realm of life. this fight will bring about far reaching consequences and changes in the whole range of life not only for ourselves but for men, children, family, church... in short for the state.
  women must make use of all media as a means of social struggle and social progress in order to free culture of male values, in the same fashion she will do this in the arts knowing that men for thousands of years were able to express herein their ideas of eroticism, sex, beauty including their mythology of vigor, energy and austerity in sculpture, paintings, novels, films, drama, drawings etc., and thereby influencing our consciousness, it will be time
AND IT IS THE RIGHT TIME.
  that women use art as a means of expression so as to influence the consciousness of all of us, let our ideas flow into the social construction of reality to create a human reality. so far the arts have

been created to a large extent solely by men. they dealt with the subjects of life, with the problems of emotional life adding only their own accounts, answers and solutions. now we must make our own assertions. we must destroy all these notions of love, faith, family, motherhood, companionship, which were not created by us and thus replace them with new ones in accordance with our sensibility, with our wishes.

to change the arts that man forced upon us means to destroy the features of woman created by man, the new values that we add to the arts will bring about new values for women in the course of the civilizing process. the arts can be of importance to the women's liberation insofar as we derive significance — our significance — from it: this spark can ignite the process of our self-determination, the question, what women can give to the arts and what the arts can give to the women, can be answered as follows: the transference of the specific situation of woman to the artistic context sets up signs and signals which provide new artistic expressions and messages on one hand, and change retrospectively the situation of women on the other.

the arts can be understood as a medium for our self-definition adding new values to the arts. these values, transmitted via the cultural sign-process, will alter reality towards an accommodation of female needs.

THE FUTURE OF WOMEN WILL BE THE HISTORY OF WOMAN.

VALIE EXPORT
Written in March 1972

WOMAN IN THE YEAR 2000 (1974)

CAROLEE SCHNEEMANN

By the year 2000 no young woman artist will meet the determined
resistance and constant undermining which I endured as a student.
Her studio and istory courses will usually be taught by women;
she will never feel like a provisional guest at the banquet of
life; or a monster defying her "God-given" role; or a belligerent
whose devotion to creativity could only exist at the expense of a
man, or men and their needs. Nor will she go into the "art world",
gracing or disgracing a pervading stud club of artists, historians,
teachers, museum directors, magazine editors, gallery dealers - all
male, or committed to masculine preserves. All that is marvelously,
already falling around our feet.

She will study art istory courses enriched by the inclusion,
discovery, and reevaluation of works by women artists: works (and
lives) until recently buried away, willfully destroyed, ignored, or
reattributed (to male artists with whom they were associated). Our
future student will be in touch with a continuous feminine creative
istory - often produced against impossible odds - from her present,
to the Renaissance and beyond. In the year 2000, books and courses
will be called "Man and His Image", "Man and His Symbols", "Art
History of Man", only to probe the source of disease and mania which
compelled patriarchal man to attribute to himself and his masculine
forebearers every invention and artifact by which civilization was
formed for over four millennia.

Our woman will have courses and books on "The Invention of
Art by Woman", "Woman - The Source of Creation", "The Matriarchal
Origins of Art", "Woman and Her Materials". Her studies of ancient
Greece and Egypt will reconcile manipulations in translation,
interpretation, and actual content of language and symbolic imagery
with the protracted and agonizing struggle between the integral,
cosmic principles of matriarchy and the aggressive man-centered
cultures gathered as the foundations of Judeo-Christian religion in
the Western world.

Fifteen years ago I told my art istory professor I thought the
bare-breasted women bull jumpers, carved in ivory or painted in
frescos about 1600 B.C. in Crete, could have been made by women
depicting women. And I considered that the preponderant neolithic
fertility figurines might have been crafted by women for themselves
- to accompany them through preganancy and birth-giving. And I
wondered if the frescos of the Mysteries, in Pompeii - almost
exclusively concerned with feminine gestures and actions - could
have been painted by women. He was shocked and annoyed, saying
that there was absolutely no authority to support such ideas.
Since then I have given myself the authority to support and

9

pursue these insights. By the year 2000 feminist archeologists, etymologists, egyptologists, biologists, sociologists will have established beyond question my contention that women determined the forms of the sacred and the functional - the divine properties of material, its religious and practical formations; that she evolved pottery, sculpture, fresco, architecture, astronomy and the laws of agriculture - all of which belonged implicitly to the female realms of transformation and production.

The shadowy notions of a harmonious core of civilisation under the aegis of the Great Mother Goddess, where the divine unity of female biological *and* imaginative creation was normal and pervasive, where the female was the source of all living and created images will once again move to clarify our own conscious desires. The sacred rituals of forming materials to embody life energies will return to the female source.

One further change will be the assembling of pioneer istorians - themselves discredited or forgotten by traditional masculine authority. In the year 2000 they will be on the required reading lists. What a joy to welcome: Helen Diner, J.J. Bachofen, Michelet, Rilke, Gould-Davis, Jane Ellen Harrison, Robert Graves, Jacquetta Hawkes, Ruth Benedict, Robert Briffault, Erich Neumann, Marie de LeCourt, Ruth Herschberger, Bryher, Hays, Mina Mosdherosch Schmidt, Clara E.C.Waters (1904), Elizabeth F. Ellet (1859).

The negative aspect is simply that the young woman coming to these vital studies will never really believe that we, in our desperate groundwork, were so crippled and isolated that a belief and dedication to a feminine istory of art was despised by those who might have taught it, and considered heretical and false by those who should have taught it. That our deepest energies were nurtured in secret, with precedents we kept secret - our lost women. Now found and to be found again.

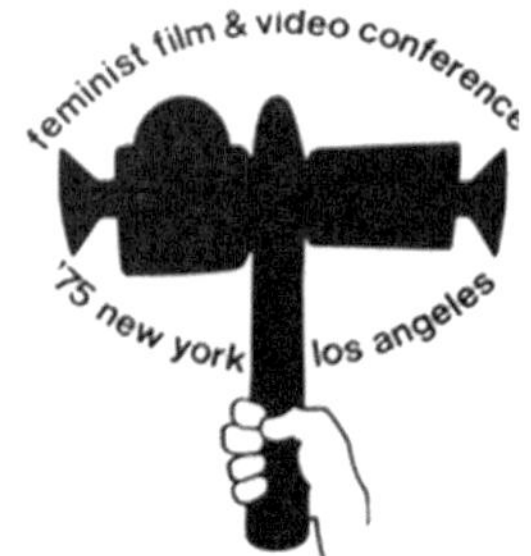

AN ON-GOING WOMANIFESTO (1975)

WRITTEN by a workgroup and ADOPTED by 80 WOMEN at
CONFERENCE of FEMINIST FILM and VIDEO
ORGANIZATIONS, NEW YORK

FEBRUARY 2, 1975

As feminists working collectively in film and video
we see our media as an ongoing process both in terms
of the way it is made and the way it is distributed
and shown. We are committed to feminist control of
the entire process. We do not accept the existing
power structure and we are committed to changing it,
by the content and structure of our images and by the
ways we relate to each other in our work and with our
audience. Making and showing our work is an ongoing
cyclical process, and we are responsible for changing
and developing our approaches as we learn from this
experience.

We see ourselves as part of the larger movement of
women dedicated to changing society by struggling
against oppression as it manifests itself in
sexism, heterosexism, racism, classism, ageism,
and imperialism. Questioning and deepening our
understanding of these works and of how language
itself can be oppressive is part of our ongoing
struggle. We want to affirm and share the positive
aspects of our experience as women in celebration.

MANIFESTO FOR A RADICAL FEMININITY
FOR AN OTHER CINEMA (1977)

MARIA KLONARIS and KATERINA THOMADAKI

> "It is within the female sex that orgasm remains the most enigmatic,
> the most inaccessible; its ultimate essence has probably
> not yet been authentically located." [1]

1. ON A FEMININE CULTURE: OBVIOUS FACTS

The existing culture is a male domineering culture, created by man for his own image / benefit.

Woman contributed to its creation, but mostly as a support for the male 'spirit'. In this culture, woman is near-absent. Unknown. Ignored. Mute. Imprisoned. Despised. Deformed. Enigmatic. Inaccessible.

In this culture, femininity is but a male projection.

The feminine culture remains to be created.

It is already being created by women unsubmissive to male order.

Through this culture alone, woman will be able to conquer the political territories necessary to her empowerment.

All woman's creative acts highlighting the distance between a general, standardised, male fabricated femininity and a self-revealed specific and unique female identity contribute to the creation of this culture.

"This said, I increasingly think that we should refrain from gendering cultural productions: this would be 'feminine', this would be 'masculine'. The issue seems different to me: it is about giving women the economic and libidinal conditions which will allow them to analyse and deconstruct social oppression and sexual repression, so that every woman may express and develop her own singularities and her own differences, as they have been produced by the risks and necessities of nature, family or society." [2]

A feminine culture can only be rupture from dominant culture.

Can only be the negation of dominant language.

Can only reject the processes of dominant art.

Can only let arise all that is oppressed by social order: body, desire, sexuality, unconscious, singularities.

Can only let the rebellion of the repressed fracture the norms of expression.

2. VISION OF A RADICAL FEMININITY

A radical femininity can only break, shatter, crush, tear apart all that weighs on her and restrains her.

Can only invent and explode.

Ripping her inventions from the depths of her own guts. Giving birth to her own identity.

A radical femininity can only be a harmony between so called feminine and masculine traits.

A symbiosis of "female" and "male" energies.

Can only be an equilibrium between the physical sex and the mental, subjective sex.

Can only bring together contradictory and / yet complementary pulsions.

A radical femininity can only be a whole – neither fragment nor lack nor deficiency.

A yoghini manifesting a serpentine energy out of her vulva.

3. PASSION FOR A RADICAL CREATION: THIS OTHER CINEMA

Unsubmissiveness. Independence. Rupture. Autonomy.

To tear apart the economic dependence of the cinema of huge crowds, huge budgets, huge means, huge consumption, huge dependency.

To tear apart the illustrative images, hostages of the social tales merchandised by the capitalist film industry.

To shatter the academicism of the gaze maintained by the industry of images.

To shatter the prefabricated notions of "real", "natural", "normal", "objective", "comprehensible" – alibis of a society which can only produce neuroses propagated by mass media.

To shatter the partition of specialisations.

To shatter hierarchies and roles.

To shatter the mirror of the fabricated woman, the passive actress, the one who obeys, the one who accepts being manipulated, the one who mediates for a stranger's orgasm.

To shatter glasses and mirrors.

I emerge.

A radical femininity can only blossom within a radical creation.

I construct my own images.

I invent my own vision, neither "natural" nor "normal" nor "objective", but real as it surges from desire, and comprehensible if one forgets whatever institutions have taught us to understand.

I free my own introspection.

I expose my roots and my sufferings: childhood, desire, revolt, repression, torture, old age, death.

I expose my archetypal and social colours: red, black, white, pink, gold, silver.

I stage my own mental structures, my geometries.

My body image imprints the film.

I open myself to you by my sentient and sensitive body. My body of woman-subject.

I offer you the rituals of my identity.

A haemorrhage of identity not mediated by anyone else, but fully asserted by myself in front of you.

I look at you.

I question you.

I give birth to an OTHER cinema.

M.K. - K.T., October 1977

1. Jacques Lacan "L'angoisse" quoted by Irène Diamantis, "Recherches sur la féminité", *Ornicar? Analytica,* vol. 5.
2. Julia Kristeva "Unes femmes" interview by Eliane Boucquey *Les Cahiers du GRIF* n° 7 (Juin 1975).

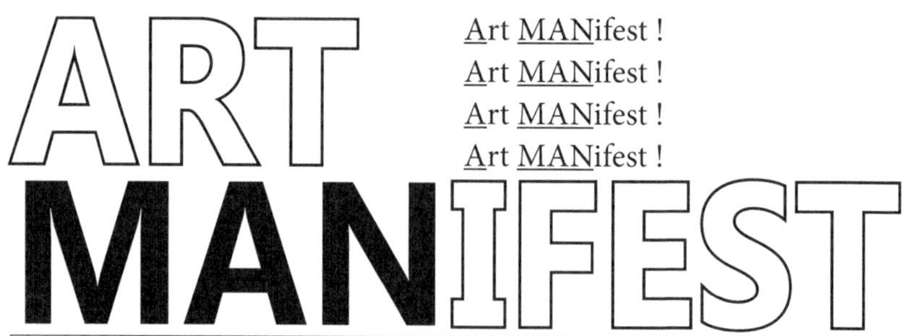

1. <u>MATERIALS</u>
HARD TECHNOLOGY RULES O.K!

2. <u>SACRIFICE</u>
SACRIFICE ALL FOR **ART**
especially SACRIFICE the WOMEN. They are the soul and substance of the EARTH
to be used up as HE makes his ART. Especially SACRIFICE the children because their
company is time consuming. They belong rightfully to the mother. ONLY biological ties
are valid. An artist cannot be sure who is his child and heir because HE is above morality ∴
children are not his responsibility. They serve only as playthings + symbols of vitality.

3. <u>CHILDREN?</u>
CHILDREN should have <u>total</u> freedom.
HE, the artist is a child in spirit ∴ HE has total freedom.

4. <u>TIME</u>
TIME is not important. HE can spend centuries thinking about 'ART'.

5. <u>ENERGY</u>
The voice of the artist - "I am strong, my energy consumes itself in the 'ART'. I suck
the world dry for my ideas.

- I am tired."

6. <u>MONEY</u>
Money is beneath my attention. Let others money-grub because <u>all</u> my resources are
spent on material for my ART.

7. <u>SPACE</u>

My need for space conquers all scruples - TO THE MOON, lads!!
My life + my ART are separate: in space, in time in energy, in emotion, in materials.
'My ART' is made in an Ivory tower.

8. <u>STATUS</u>
   'ART' is special
   'ART' is novelty
   'ARt' is solitary
   'ARt' is IMPORTANT!
   'ART' is <u>large</u> !

ARTS FEMINISTO ①

---

1. <u>MATERIALS</u>

Make it in knitting; use Aunt Maude's curtains; crotchet it; use your own brains; draw it in the road; paint the town etc etc and so on. Soft technology = Accessibility. Use the wonders of Woolworths - look in yer bin; objets trouve; loosely translated = in yr. head

---

2. <u>SACRIFICE</u>

If poetry comes not as naturally as the leaves in a tree, it had better not come at all.
SHE refuses martyrdom.
MOTHER and CHILD are not one word.
SACRIFICE is useless (We tried it for 20 centuries + it doesn't work)
- sacrifice <u>NOTHING</u> - include it instead.

---

3. <u>CHILDREN</u>

CHILDREN can be taught to be responsive.
SHE, the artist, is a responsive adult ∴ SHE is responsible.

---

4. <u>TIME</u>

TIME is precious. We work hard and we <u>create</u> time.

---

5. <u>ENERGY</u>

Our energy is shared for people. With others we can make art works out of our own selves as the spider spins her web from her own body.

---

6. <u>MONEY</u>

Our children must eat. We feed them with our blood and our breasts. We are creative. We know how the artworks are made.

---

7. <u>SPACE</u>

We are EARTH. Space is our mind. WE have no need to RACE.
Do NOT spacerace/rape my moon sister!
We do it in the road!

---

8. <u>STATUS</u>

Art is like cooking. Art is like childbirth.
Art is like breathing. Our Art is ancient magic.
Art is <u>solidarity</u>. Our artwork is together even when we are apart.
Ours is ordinary + useful magic.
We don't BOAST.

This statement was not designed as such but as a letter to comfort my friend Catherine Nicholson because she was thinking that what she does is not 'proper Art'.
I read it aloud later at a meeting of Women Artists in Scunthorpe and it seemed generally appropriate to the exhibition so we included it. I think the title explains itself 'Arts MANifest versus FEMINISTO', but sometimes people only read the left hand column and misunderstand completely. It should be read as opposite statements of two conflicting philosophies of art.

To whom it may concern, a few words about 'CONTENT' or 'SUBJECT MATTER' or "I does it 'cos I does it, don't I?"

"Men have too often wanted to attain immortality as the content and scope of their lives. Here they started a dangerous game which they are forced to continue by defending <u>competition</u>, <u>superiority</u> and <u>ambition</u> as positive and outstanding values.

Women are outsiders. We expressed our disapproval and looked for other more possible solutions, often improving them. Since then, we have carried the weight of our decision - inferiorization.

We are not at the point in which we can openly manifest our own concept in human relationships. This may seem new for the world around us but we can now express a reality that has <u>been ignored</u> and despised for too long and finally live in another dimension."

Suzanne Santoro 'Towards New Expression'
Rome 1972 (Rivolta Feminista)

51% of the wor[ld] population have [not] spoken yet. There [is] AN OTHER reality. t[his] can be our subject.

Competition/Superiority/Ambition?*!?!!

Just ask yourself why 'Abstract Expressionism' has become so played out, so hollow of meanin[g] up a blind alley. Or think of how 'artists' play to the 'gallery'. Artists singing a tune, to which ONL[Y] the initiated (usually other artists) know the words? Think of what used to be called the 'Alternativ[e] Society', and how it has evolved its alternative Barons and Dukes; its alternative con men; alternativ[e] crooks and robbers and murderers. Alternative <u>Everything</u> that is just as horrific as straight societ[y] and then ask yourself did it do women much good? "Where does the competition etc go to i[n] "Alternative ways of life?"
SOMETHING HAS BEEN MISSING, GUESS WHAT? <u>NO PRIZES</u> for the answe[r] It's not competition.   It's not a COMPETITION.   IT'S <u>NOT</u> A COMPETITION!!!

9. <u>CONCLUSION</u>
The artwork will BE invented which will fit tenderly around the needs of women and children.
<u>SHE</u> will invent it - (<u>AGAIN</u>) !

I have no patience with blokes who say "The subject matter of art is ART" etc....

competition
superiority
ambition

?
I refuse to compete because I don't need to be a 'winner' or a 'loser'. Competition is irrelevant because the real issue is effective communication.

?
Elitism is an example of how societies exclude most humans from participation and full development. Superiority/inferiority is irrelevant because listening to each other is more important. Ideas are NOT to be confused with private property.

?
Ambition to what end?
Ambition to dominate by fame

intellect } all redundant in a Feminist
wealth } art because recognition is immediate international and profound, if you are personal AND universal at the same time. Women <u>are able to do this</u> at this stage in history because we have profound similarities in our experiences

This <u>NEW CONTENT</u> will, at first look bizarre, rather like looking at something familiar from the other side. The dark side of the moon. The view from the other side of underneath. People will be sometimes bewildered or simply be able to ignore it, because in some ways it will use the same imagery and materials that we have been used to, but in <u>another</u> mode of expression, but MANY MANY FEMALES OF <u>ALL SEXES</u> WILL RECOGNISE IT. Accusations of banality will probably be rife, because in a technology dominated by reverence for <u>innovation</u>, <u>evolution</u> (using materials not damaging to the ecology) is suspected of being <u>non-creative</u> in other words, current ideas of what is 'creative' and 'passive' will be challenged, but possibly obliquely, by implication.

FIRST MANIFESTO ON THE CULTURAL REVOLUTION OF WOMEN (1978)

the witch-mothers

feminist witch-mothers are women who seek the feminine principle within themselves and feel conjoined with the triple creatress as daughters.

religion and politics are interdependent.

we believe that at a time when we are fighting for the right to control our own bodies, it is also time to fight for the well-being of our souls.

we believe that in addition to the fight for our rights, which will last for generations, we must also find a way to continually replenish our positive energies. we believe that without a secure foundation in the spiritual realm, there can be no progress for us.

we believe that we are part of a changing universal consciousness that was predetermined thousands of years ago in the age of the matriarchies.

we believe that the renewed development of feminine creativity and power will engender new strength for a humane development of our society.

we commit ourselves to living our lives in love of ourselves and our sisters.

we are conjoined with joy, self-love and self-assertion.

we commit ourselves to vindicating our interests and those of our sisters by learning the magic arts: through blessing, through punishing, through healing, and through the inclusion of what is insufficiently rooted in our community identified by women.

women's magic is not only a religion. it is a way of living. in the cults of the mother, the magic of women was general knowledge. it was information about how women can live freely on this planet. rediscovering this capability is one of the important contributions that women of the feminist movement have to give.

we must learn how we can trust our soul by learning that our right to own it is rooted in our consciousness of the goddess, the feminine principle of the universe, and in ourselves.

this is the source of our independence.
we are prepared to battle those who are simplistic.
we are equal and committed to contributing to political,
communal and personal solutions.
we are committed to teaching women how they can organise
themselves as witch-mothers and will share our traditions with
them.
we deny men the teaching of our magic.
Our immediate goal is to assemble with one another according to
our old laws of women and to remember our past, to renew our
power, and to affirm our goddess of the ten-thousand names.

ZSE BUDAPEST
ULRIKE ROSENBACH
SUSAN B. ANTHONY COVEN

CHANGE, MY PROBLEM IS A PROBLEM OF A WOMAN (1979)

EWA PARTUM

A woman lives in a social structure that is alien to her. Its model, superannuated in relation to her current role, was created by and for men. A woman can operate in a social structure that is alien to her if she masters the discipline of camouflage and leaves out her own personality. At the moment of discovering her own awareness, possibly having little in common with the realities of her current life, a social and cultural problem arises. Not fitting into the social structure created for her, she will create a new one. This possibility of discovering the self and the authenticity of her own experiences, work on her own problems and awareness through the very specific experience of being a woman in a patriarchal society in a world that is alien to the self, is the problem of what is called 'feminist art'. It is the motivation for creating art for a woman artist. The phenomenon of feminist art reveals to a woman her new role, the possibility of self-realisation.

WOMEN ARTISTS OF PAKISTAN MANIFESTO (1983)

We, the women artists of Pakistan,

having noted with concern the decline in the
status and conditions of life of Pakistani women; and

having noted the adverse effects of the anti-reason, anti-
arts environment on the quality of life in our homeland; and

having noted the significant contribution the pioneering
women artists have made to the cause of arts and art
education in Pakistan and

believing as we do in the basic rights of all men, women
and children to a life free from want and enriched by the
joys of fruitful labour and cultural self-realisation; and
our commitment, as practitioners and teachers of the arts,
to the noblest ideals of a free, rational and civilised
existence:

affirm the following principles to guide us in our struggle for the
cultural development of our people to serve as the manifesto of
the women artists of Pakistan:

1. We acknowledge the outstanding contribution made by women
    artists to the conservation and promotion of the artistic
    genius of our people and their role in pioneering art
    education in the country; we salute them for this and for their
    determination to spread out at all levels of education and to
    all strata of society.

2. We unreservedly support the Pakistani women's struggle for
    equality of rights, status, and dignity with menfolk.

3. We call upon women engaged in any creative field in Pakistan to
    stand together for the cause of women's emancipation not only from
    all constraints, perpetrated in the name of law and morality, but
    also from all forms of prejudice, superstition and cant.

4. We recognise, respect and uphold the right of every woman
    artist to her own faith, her individual approach to content,
    form, medium, method, technique and style in the realisation
    of her artistic ideals. And we denounce any attempt, overt or
    covert, to suppress, inhibit, control or regiment her artistic
    functioning, or to interfere otherwise, with her basic right to
    freedom of expression.

5. We vigorously condemn the attitude which minimises woman's
    constructive role in society, and attempts to restrict her
    active and rightful participation in society.

6. We condemn the attitude which distorts the original and age-
    old role of woman as the giver and sustainer of life, love and
    affection and vulgarises it into an image of obscenity.

7. We call upon all women artists to take their place in the
    vanguard of the Pakistani women's struggle to retain their
    pristine image and their rightful place in society.

    So that we may replace in the lives of our people
    despair with hope, brutality with compassion, darkness with
    light, and anarchy with culture, and leave the world a
    happier, more beautiful and more peaceful a place than we
    found it.

    Signed by 15 Women Artists in Lahore - 1983

1. Rabia Zuberi   10. Birjees Iqbal

2. Abbasi Abidi   11. Riffat Alvi

3. Mamoona Bashir   12. Meher Afroz

4. Salima Hashmi   13. Nahid

5. Lala Rukh   14. Qudsia Nisar

6. Talat Ahmad   15. Veeda Ahmed

7. Zubeda Javed

8. Sheherezade Alam

9. Jalees Nagi

15

THERE HAVE ALWAYS BEEN GREAT BLACKWOMEN ARTISTS
(1986)

CHILA KUMARI BURMAN

We face many problems when trying to establish the very existence of Blackwomen's art, and a strong social and political base from which to develop our study of it. Firstly, we have to struggle to establish our existence, let alone our credibility as autonomous beings, in the art world. Secondly, we can only retain that credibility and survive as artists if we become fully conscious of ourselves, lest we are demoralised or weakened by the social, economic, and political constraints which the white-male art establishment imposes and will continue to impose on us.

This paper, then, is saying Blackwomen artists are here, we exist and we exist positively, despite the racial, sexual and class oppressions which we suffer, but first, however, we must point out the way in which these oppressions have operated in a wider context – not just in the art worlds, but also in the struggles for black and female liberation.

It is true to say that although Blackwomen have been the staunchest allies of black men and white women in the struggle against the oppression we all face at the hands of the capitalist and patriarchal system, we have hardly ever received either the support we need or recognition of our pivotal role in this struggle. Blackwomen now realise that because of the specific ways in which we are oppressed by white-male dominated society, we must present a new challenge to imperialism, racism and sexism from inside and outside the established black liberation movement. It is this realisation which has a lot to do with many second generation British Blackwomen reclaiming art, firstly as a legitimate area of activity for Blackwomen as a distinct group of people, secondly as a way of developing awareness (denied us by the racist, sexist, class society) of ourselves as complete human beings, and thirdly as a contribution to the black struggle in general.

Having said this, Blackwomen's ability to do any or all of these three things is restricted by the same pressures of racism, sexism and class exclusivity which we experience in society in general, The bourgeois art establishment only acknowledges white men as truly creative and innovative artists, whilst recognising art by white women only as a homogenous expression of femininity and art by black people (or, more accurately, within the terms of reference used, black men as a static expression of the ritual experience of the daily lives of their communities, be they in the Third World or the imperialist hinterland. In this system of knowledge, Blackwomen artists, quite simply, do not exist.

Nevertheless, if we look at the way in which these assumptions have been challenged to date, particularly by white women, we can see nothing that acknowledges that Blackwomen exist. Art history is an academic subject, studied in patriarchal art institutions, and white middle-class women have used their advantageous class position to gain access to these institutions by applying pressure to them in a way which actually furthers the exclusion of black artists in general. White women's failure to inform themselves of the obstacles faced by black artists and in particular Blackwomen artists has lead to the production of an extremely Eurocentric theory and practice of 'women's art'. It seems that white feminists, as much as white women in general, either do not attempt or find it difficult to conceive of Blackwomen's experience. Some of those who do not attempt to may claim that they cannot speak for Blackwomem, but this is merely a convenient way of sidestepping their own racism. The fact remains that in a patriarchal and sexist society, all black people suffer from racism, and it is quite possible for white women to turn racism, which stems from patriarchy, to their advantage. Black men are unable to do this and, theoretically, are unable to turn sexism to their advantages, although they can do this for short-term gains which in the long term will never benefit black people as a whole. This has happened to a certain extent in the art world, where black men have failed to recognise Blackwomen artists or have put pressure on us to produce certain kinds of work linked to a male-dominated notion of struggle. However, because of their race and class position, black men have been unable to use the resources of information in art institutions in the same way white middle-class women have.

The struggles of Blackwomen artists

The first stage of most Blackwomen artists' encounter with the art establishment is their entry into art college. There are hardly any Blackwomen attending art college in Britain, and those who do, according to a survey of Blackwomen artists I carried out, seem to have experienced a mixture of hostility and indifference from their college. Because their white tutors work within an imperial art tradition, using the aesthetic conventions of the dominant ideology, they are unwilling to come to terms with Blackwomen students and their work. This resistance manifests itself in many ways – some Blackwomen art students have found themselves asking why they as individuals found it easy to get into art college, only to realise that they are there purely as tokens, and in general it appears that Blackwomen's very presence in white-male art institutions is frequently called into question. Apart from denying us the support and encouragement that white art students receive, art colleges make us feel as though we don't belong inside their walls by the way in which our work is looked at. Those of us who have done more overtly political work have made white tutors very uncomfortable and, as a result, hostile, whilst students who have done less obviously challenging work have been questioned for not producing the kind of work which tutors expect black people to produce. Class differences amongst Blackwomen are significant here, for working-class Blackwomen have generally been quicker to reject the ideology of the art establishment and have therefore found it difficult to accept any kind of token status or to produce work of a more acceptable nature. Those who have not taken such an oppositional stance have still suffered from having their work analysed within a very narrow framework because their tutors have expected them to produce 'ethnic' work which reflects their 'cultural origin' using, for example, 'bright carnival colours', and white tutors and students alike have expressed confusion when such work has not been forthcoming. Another tendency of white tutors, irrespective of the work they are presented with, is to discuss art from the third world with Blackwomen in a patronising and racist manner.

Of course, the assumption that Blackwomen will produce work with 'ethnic' or 'primitive' associations is one that white tutors make about black men as well, but it is important to point out that male and female white tutors are more inclined to see black men as having a more prominent role in this misconceived tradition. One Blackwoman student at Bradford art college commented:

> Funny how they always refer to you as some sort of bridge or crossing point between two things. Black meets woman. That's handy. As if you don't have an experience which is your own, but borrow from the brothers and sisters in struggle.

It seems, then, that when art colleges and universities give places to Blackwomen, which in itself is a rare event, all the forces of the dominant aesthetic ideology are brought to bear on us. Blackwomen artists are ignored, isolated, described as 'difficult', slotted into this or that stereotype and generally discouraged in every conceivable way from expressing ourselves in the way we want to. This system of oppression and exclusion extends well beyond our time as art students. There are no full-time lecturing posts at art colleges and universities filled by Blackwomen in the entire country - instead we are offered 'freelance' work as visiting lecturers, which will never be enough to initiate a critique of contemporary art practice which is so desperately needed in every single art department in the country.

In addition, Blackwomen artists are denied the opportunity to develop their work as individuals to develop their work as individuals in the same way that white artists can through grants from sources such as the Arts Council, the Greater London Council, regional arts associations and the Calouste Gulbenkian Foundation. Even through some of these sources such as the GLC and the Greater London Arts Association have recently begun to realise how much they have neglected Black visual arts, on the only occasion that a Blackwoman had received funding from the GLC as an individual, this has still been on unsatisfactory terms which differ significantly from the terms on which the only black man in this position has been funded. The man in question has been funded without any preconditions except that he produces a certain amount of work, whilst, the

woman was funded by the Arts and Recreation Department of the GLC for
a year on the condition that she was attached to a community arts centre has
a 'community artist', and the stipulation was made that work she produced
should not reflect her desires as an individual but the interests of the 'black
community' of the experience of an individual Blackwomen and had funded
her on the basis of an historical notion of 'community' or 'ethnic minority'
art, but when it came to applying for the Arts Council, it appeared that the
role she has been pushed into was not individual enough . The rejection of
her application to this body read:

> We do not think that your proposed project fits the terms of reference
> for this training scheme which is specifically aimed at developing the
> individual's skills, and is not to assist with research projects.

If even the GLC funded a Blackwoman artist only as a 'community artist',
this illustrates our position in a kind of funding no-woman's-land, because the
Arts Council, racist and sexist as it is already, will continue to see our work
as unfundable research projects and, as was the case with the application
mentioned, refer us to bodies such as the Association of the Commonwealth
Universities, further relegating us to the marginality of the 'ghetto artist',
completely outside the mainstream British art world.

Blackwomen artists fight back

The resilience of Blackwomen in the face of oppression has manifested
itself in the art world through our ability to produce and exhibit work despite
all the social, economic and political constraints described above. The first
all-Blackwomen's show at the Africa Centre in 1983 was not just a beginning;
Blackwomen artists have been actively involved in exhibitions with white
artists and Black men artists for several years, but this all-Blackwomen's
show and the ones that have taken place since then – Blackwoman Time
Now, 1985 International Women's Day Show, Mirror Reflecting Darkly,
etc.- represent a significant new direction which has much to do with the
development of what Barbara Smith describes as 'our own intellectual
traditions'.

It is obvious that the majority of Black artists see their work in
opposition to the establishment view of art as something that is 'above'
politics, and Blackwomen artists see their work as integral to the struggles
of Blackwomen and black people in general, but although Blackwomen's
own culture plays a large part in determining the culture and form of our
work, we often concentrate on different issues to black men, who, as one
Blackwoman artist points out, often believe that 'artists who are making
through their works a collective, aggressive challenge to cultural domination
are "real" black artists and making Black Art. But some male artists fail to
go through to assert their identity and survive'.

Alice Walker illustrates the difference between these two ideas of Black Art in 'In Search for Our Mothers' Gardens' and goes on to put forward an alternative way for the black artist to operate:

> I am impressed by people who claim they can see everything and event in strict terms of black and white but their work is not, in my long contemplated and earnestly considered opinion, either black or white, but a dull, uniform gray. It is boring because it is easy and requires only that the reader be a lazy reader and a prejudiced one. Each story or poem has a formula usually two-thirds 'hate whitey's guts' and one third 'I am black, beautiful and almost always right'. Art is not flattery, and the work of every artist must be more difficult than that.
> My major advice to young black artists would be that they shut themselves up somewhere away from all the debates about who they are and what colour they are and just turn out paintings and poems and stories and novels. Of course the kind of artist we are required to be cannot do this (our people are waiting).

Alice Walker's advice is important here, for she is not suggesting that we cut ourselves off from the outside world, because we cannot forget the mark our oppression as black women have made on us, or the fact that 'our people are waiting'. The point is that what we need as artists is the opportunity to create the situation she describes so that we are allowed to develop an understanding of ourselves and of the struggle we have to wage within British society for recognition and respect. If we are able to do this by having adequate resources put at our disposal, we hope to share our experiences with, awaken the consciousness of and impart our strength to the whole society.

Feminist Manifesto

Gisela Breitling
November 1989*

I

Many of the ingredients that make up our present way of thinking, all those ideas and dogmas that have been prescribed as indispensable and as propellants of progress, which we have swallowed whole in the belief that we could not live without them lest we fall behind, are now being recognized as oppressive relics from the nineteenth century, inherited dregs that are still oozing from the landfills of that time.

1.   The Myth of Independent Research

Now that the scientific revolution is in process of devouring its own offspring it has become clear that its direction was never determined by any pure striving for knowledge. The act of attaching research to a life-destroying mania for growth is a logical consequence of detaching it from ethical considerations, an act that was presented as "freedom". The idea that the urge to explore leads to humanitarian progress proves to be a chimera. Yet people continue to bet on that Trojan horse, even though it is well known that the advocates of club law are concealed within it and are asserting the pre-legal injustice of the stronger – the maxims that humans can produce anything they're able to imagine (to the point that they have long since ceased being able to imagine what they produce), and that they are entitled to do anything they're capable of doing – are even obliged to do it – purely on the grounds that they can.

2.   The Myth of Autonomous Nation States

In the age of giant corporations, large-scale research, universal satellite-supported television coverage, geostrategic data transfer, global pollution and individual as well as general mobility (whether voluntary or forced), nation states have become fiction, fossils of bygone eras. Their border fortifications and defence apparatuses are as obsolete as the belief that citizenship conveys any natural sense of identity. Highly developed industrial nations cannot be defended militarily; they are too fragile and too susceptible to disruption. If the main artery, electricity, were cut, or if chemical factories and nuclear power plants were blown up, they would simply collapse. That said, there's little to be gained from a non-military assault. Resuscitation attempts would be far too costly. So, it is no longer appropriate to stake the claims of power with a marshal's baton. The military has long ceased to serve purposes of national defence and it has turned into an institutionalised threat, both external and internal – the latter to keep the country's inhabitants in check should this be required.

3.   The Myth of the Free Market
The era of early capitalism is an object lesson in the free play of economic forces. Proof that these forces do not, in fact, regulate themselves and must be controlled to mitigate the worst excesses of their "play instinct" has long been established. The boastful notion that in the absence of state planning and intervention, a capitalist economy merely follows supply and demand, and that this leads to an optimal distribution of capacities and goods, is currently being played off against the manifest disaster of the socialist planned economy. At the same time, state control of the free-market profit motive is currently producing new catastrophes and absurdities that are being lost from view: subsidy policies and misguided planning have resulted in a grotesque, unimaginable waste of raw materials and energy: mountains of butter, lakes of milk and wine, gross overproduction of electricity, the annual destruction of tons of agricultural products, monocultures that destroy entire regions, over-fertilisation and excessive exploitation of the soil on the one hand, and the desertification of agricultural land that has been cultivated for centuries on the other.

The fact that a socialist planned economy has been irrevocably recognised as a failure, and that some capitalist market economies in western industrialised countries have led to a better general supply should not be used to gloss over the realities of capitalist legitimacy. The systems and worldviews of the two previously hostile power blocs have proven themselves to be more or less ineffectual simplifications that are not adequate to the complex challenges of the technical-industrial world.

II
Freedom rather than socialism? Whose freedom? Socialism as freedom? Where is freedom to be found, and who, exactly, is free? It was sought and promised, yet it was never our freedom. Our freedom was not on the agenda because the oldest monopoly over opinion is held independently of power blocs and military alliances. Rather, it is preserved in legal systems and religions – and consists of

the dominance of the male over the female sex. For millennia, the issuances and emissaries of this imbalance have poisoned all the ideologies, all postulates of freedom as well as all downfalls. What is distinctive as well as especially pernicious about this form of rule is its unsurpassed method of secrecy. Nowhere else has this been achieved so perfectly. Patriarchal rule remains a secret even when it is openly and publicly discussed, because this global form of domination has been declared a private matter, an internal family affair.

Patriarchy, with a shrewdness that is typical of the logic of power, has posited the family as the nucleus of the state. The family constitutes a legal vacuum, where there is no division of power. Club law applies here. And not only does it apply, it is also practised. The women's shelters and sexually abused daughters attest to what has been suppressed for a long time. But of course, club law also applies when it is not being exercised. And the psychological consequences of this legal constellation are an even better kept secret. Within the nucleus of the family, the ugly and hateful acts of domination and subjugation are practised on a model scale, in vitro, so to speak. On a 1:1 scale, they then come to be called colonialism, racism, exploitation, physical extermination. All legal systems, social orders and sciences, all world views and ideologies to date have always produced both: self-importance along with subservience, infantile demands for service along with servility, fantasies of omnipotence, mendacity, notorious arrogance along with cowardice, an exaggerated sense of entitlement and lack of autonomy, self-satisfied swagger and lack of self – and hatred and contempt on both sides.

The 200 years since the French Revolution have shown that human rights are essentially men's rights, that human beings at best become brothers while refraining from annihilating each other in fratricidal wars. The forty years since the founding of the two German states, each celebrating itself as a pinnacle of social progress on German soil, demonstrate that they – like all other states past and present – were built on a foundation of gender apartheid.

Admittedly, the Iron Curtain has been perforated, and the Berlin wall, that monument to pan-German cement-headedness, is among the collapsing new institutions. Admittedly, witnessing a new political movement in the GDR fills us with enthusiasm and admiration. We hear and greatly esteem the call for freedom and self-determination. It is a noble call. Yet by issuing the same call, we have been putting our reputation on the line for the past twenty years. We have a bad reputation – because we are feminists. Apparently, the call for freedom and self-determination acquires a bad taste when vocalized by women, not shoulder to shoulder with male comrades in the name of male interests, but in their own name and their own interests. In that case, the call apparently merits neither empathy nor respect. Women's call for their own freedom and self-determination somehow becomes offensive.

History shows that no revolution has ever succeeded without women and that women have been at the front lines of every revolution – and this from the very beginning… until the gentlemen negotiated a new power arrangement. When in past revolutions it was a case of all or nothing, when the brothers united as brothers because they had nothing to lose but their chains, and called their sisters to their side or tolerated them at their side, then, as soon as the slightest success was won, they kept it all for themselves, leaving nothing for their sisters but the snares with which they have always held down the female sex. And there always were enough patient, solicitous souls among their sisters who rushed to the kitchens and used their hard-won laurels to spice the roast for their freedom-hungry brothers. And there were always enough quick-tongued women who burnt their mouths in calling for freedom and who hurriedly preached silence, patience and a new femininity to their sisters. The brothers' freedom has always cost the sisters dear, since it came at the expense of their own.

III

Our patience with this type of femininity and masculinity is exhausted. We are no longer prepared to join united fraternal fronts; we no longer join in when they preach freedom. It never was freedom in our sense. And neither do we excuse the many delicate attempts at pacification any longer. We do not want a gender-specific general amnesty for women – it is too deeply entangled in the corruption scandals of male power and bribery. Neither do we share the presumption of innocence based on gender characteristics.

We want to do what we think is right. We want to decide about our own lives and about the affairs of the society in which we live. We want to walk with our heads held high and our backs straight.

"We are the people!" This call does not have a rousing, majestic or revolutionary sound for us. Rather, the phrase "the people" fills us with apprehension. Who are the people? No sooner do the people make their voices heard than they shout "fatherland".

Since time immemorial, it has been the fathers who agreed in the fatherlands that their rights and freedoms should apply. The pinnacle of freedom was thought to have been attained when these rights and freedoms were not just reserved for the few but intended to apply to all the fathers in principle.

Are women included in "the people"? To date, women have been treated as subordinates. They had and continue to have limited rights in the fatherlands, especially when they wish to or are required to go to a country that is not the homeland of their fathers. Women have no nation; they are international.

Both liberal democracy of the Western European kind and the socialism of the East Bloc have done their part in making the rule of men over women invisible. The idea of equal rights for women has come to mean that no more fuss should be made about gender. And the permission granted to some women to participate in male science, male professions and even male politics has blindsided many supporters of women to the growing, assimilatory power of patriarchy.

IV

At present there is so much talk of "WE" that we are sceptical. Who is meant by this "we" – whom does it include and exclude? With its appropriating intentions, "we" achieves the same unjust distribution that is familiar from the economy: privatisation of profit and socialisation of loss – physical, spiritual and monetary gains are credited to the protagonists while the minions bear the loss. The historical balance sheets add up to an overall debt in terms of past and present disasters as well as of the uncovered bills of the future, while the stimulating cultural and social profits are appropriated by individual men.

Incorporating women into the "we", whether this be a "we" of guilt or of pride, is therefore inadmissible. Even if women, and more particularly white women of white men, benefit from some of the fruits of male efforts, this does not give the man the right to incorporate women into his "we" by virtue of such a bribe. Neither does the woman, who has always suffered as a result of male efforts, have any right to associate her own marginalisation with the moral privilege of innocence.

The demand to abolish male gender privilege must be made independently of any appropriation as well as independently of any gender-based guilt or innocence. It must result from the realisation that society must of necessity be an equal and inclusive whole. It must arise both independently and outside of individual experience, which tends to dismiss male gender privilege as a "women's problem" – since it can hardly be that. Just as anti-capitalism is not a matter of the poor, medicine a matter of the sick, housing a problem of the homeless and anti-Semitism a problem of the Jews, male domination is not a women's problem – or a problem of women who are not well off, or even of women who can't get along with men. Neither can responsibility simply be disowned under the motto 'I'm fine, I don't have a problem with it', whether this be uttered by women or men. By conceding that no one gives up privileges voluntarily, women have given men carte blanche, and men have gladly used this as an excuse to sit back and relax. But it is an assertion that has been disproved a thousand times over – people, both men and women, have given up privileges and even their lives for the sake of their convictions and realisations, without speculating on any reward. Further, the abolition of male domination is not just about privilege. The abolition of male-determined monopoly society requires the creation of a new identity, which transcends gender definitions that have prevailed until now for both women and men.

Women have always had the courage to transgress such definitions, preferring to pay the price of freedom rather than the price of bondage. And the courage to find a new identity includes the courage to face loneliness, for men no less than women. Because the feminist revolution is radical dissent. Yes indeed, feminism really is the final straw – that is, the last possible, final experiment in the human experiment.

Note:
* This manifesto emerged from a discussion with a working group from the "Council of Women" in Berlin, in which Halina Bendkowski, Pieke Biermann, Sabine Bohle, Hannelore May, Irene Stoehr and Christina Thürmer-Rohr were involved.

RIOT GRRL MANIFESTO *(1991)*

BECAUSE us girls crave records and books and fanzines that speak to US that WE feel included in and can understand in our own ways.

BECAUSE we wanna make it easier for girls to see/hear each other's work so that we can share strategies and criticize-applaud each other.

BECAUSE we must take over the means of production in order to create our own meanings.

BECAUSE viewing our work as being connected to our girlfriends-politics-real lives is essential if we are gonna figure out how we are doing impacts, reflects, perpetuates, or DISRUPTS the status quo.

BECAUSE we recognize fantasies of Instant Macho Gun Revolution as impractical lies meant to keep us simply dreaming instead of becoming our dreams AND THUS seek to create revolution in our own lives every single day by envisioning and creating alternatives to the bullshit christian capitalist way of doing things.

BECAUSE we want and need to encourage and be encouraged in the face of all our own insecurities, in the face of beergutboyrock that tells us we can't play our instruments, in the face of "authorities" who say our bands/zines/etc are the worst in the US and

BECAUSE we don't wanna assimilate to someone else's (boy) standards of what is or isn't.

BECAUSE we are unwilling to falter under claims that we are reactionary "reverse sexists" AND NOT THE TRUEPUNKROCKSOULCRUSADERS THAT WE KNOW we really are.

BECAUSE we know that life is much more than physical survival and are patently aware that the punk rock "you can do anything" idea is crucial to the coming angry grrrl rock revolution which seeks to save the psychic and cultural lives of girls and women everywhere, according to their own terms, not ours.

BECAUSE we are interested in creating non-heirarchical ways of being AND making music, friends, and scenes based on communication + understanding, instead of competition + good/bad categorizations.

BECAUSE doing/reading/seeing/hearing cool things that validate and challenge us can help us gain the strength and sense of community that we need in order to figure out how bullshit like racism, able-bodieism, ageism, speciesism, classism, thinism, sexism, anti-semitism and heterosexism figures in our own lives.

BECAUSE we see fostering and supporting girl scenes and girl artists of all kinds as integral to this process.

BECAUSE we hate capitalism in all its forms and see our main goal as sharing information and staying alive, instead of making profits of being cool according to traditional standards.

BECAUSE we are angry at a society that tells us Girl = Dumb, Girl = Bad, Girl = Weak.

BECAUSE we are unwilling to let our real and valid anger be diffused and/or turned against us via the internalization of sexism as witnessed in girl/girl jealousism and self defeating girltype behaviors.

BECAUSE I believe with my wholeheartmindbody that girls constitute a revolutionary soul force that can, and will change the world for real.

THE MANIFESTO: EVA AND CO. (1992)

Eva and Co. has chosen to take her own life!

- Eva and Co. has sinned. Against our better judgement, we have kept up too long with our non-conformist market attempts. Ten years Eva and Co – women´s artist´s group and feminist cultural magazine are enough! (or too much?)

- Eva and Co. takes the first step; other institutions could follow us! Many of them are overdue and continue to exist only because they are too cowardly to draw the obvious conclusions from their paradoxical and unproductive work. Women are braver!
We no longer secretly ask ourselves: for what?

- The magazine Eva and Co. was expensive and elitist. We did not manage to make a mass circulation magazine out of it. Consumption is everything – as digestible and entertaining as possible, open to everyone, not too demanding and please, not too serious!

- Eva and Co. served as the token presence of women in the art world. We are no longer the token! It is everyone´s responsibility that women appear more in the public domain.

- Besides: art is not wanted! You make yourself an enemy of the people. Official support barely keeps us alive. But one gets the impression that the officials themselves don´t know exactly why, and that they are only too cowardly to cut off the supply of money.

- An enemy of the state as decoration? Art as a piece of jewelry for politicians, fashionable urban citizens and image conscious companies. Art as enticement for streams of tourists. Graz as cultural city.

- The content of art, the subversive, the revolutionary, the questioning is silenced. Instead, formalities, cliches like "freedom of expression", the art market, etc. are discussed.

- We know about our so-called artistic freedom to do as we please, but we no longer want to be the fools. We are serious about content.

- Today everything is valued through money. What we are doing obviously has no value – we draw the conclusions. Art is valuable only as an object of speculative investment.

- We reject art! Women, stop producing art, it is pointless! Remember: women´s art is not in! The racism proliferating everywhere demands its victims. We are not the first!

- We refuse to continue creating art! Parties are cheaper and you can use something else for decoration.

- Success killed us. And not only us – but we won´t allow it to bureaucratize us, to burn us out or to pacify us!

- Art should be a laboratory. The importance of an experimental stage has to be recognized and promoted. It is necessary for every innovation and indispensable for surviving.

- We demand diversity of art and not official decisions about what art is.

- Art is political and socially relevant.

- Women artists are supposed to be perfect housewives, organizers, managers, gallery owners, etc. Enough! In the future, men will be allowed to organize; we will focus on our art.

- It is not sufficient to organize women artists in associations. We will develop better strategies and form ourselves anew! We will infiltrate everything! We will go underground and to the sky. And be warned: in the future we will camouflage ourselves.

- From now on we will again give free rein to our madness.

- Women artists will be as present everywhere as in Eva and Co.

- Thus we demand: Only women´s art for the next ten years!

31. 12. 1992
Eva and Co.
We were: Eva Ursprung, Veronika Dreier, Erika Thümmel, Reni Hofmüller.

BITCH MUTANT MANIFESTO (1994)

VNS MATRIX

The atomic wind catches your wings and you are propelled backwards into the
future, an entity time travelling through the late C20th, a space case, an alien angel
maybe, looking down the deep throat of a million catastrophes.

screenflash of a millionmillion conscious machines
burns brilliant
users caught in the static blitz of carrier fire
unseeing the download that scribbles on their burntout retinas
seize in postreal epileptic bliss
eat code and die

Sucked in, down through a vortex of banality. You have just missed the twentieth
century. You are on the brink of the millenium - which one - what does it matter?
It's the cross dissolve that's captivating. The hot contagion of millenia fever fuses
retro with futro, catapulting bodies with organs into technotopia . . . where code
dictates pleasure and satisfies desire.

Pretty pretty applets adorn my throat. I am strings of binary. I am pure artifice.
Read only my memories. Upload me into your pornographic imagination. Write me.
Identity explodes in multiple morphings and infiltrates the system at root.

Unnameable parts of no whole short circuit the code recognition programs flipping
surveillance agents into hyperdrive which spew out millions of bits of corrupt
data as they seize in fits of schizophrenic panic and trip on terror. So what's the
new millenium got to offer the dirty modemless masses? Ubiquitous fresh water?
Simulation has its limits. Are the artists of oppressed nations on a parallel agenda?
Perhaps it is just natural selection?

The net's the parthenogenetic bitch-mutant feral child of big daddy mainframe.
She's out of of control, kevin, she's the sociopathic emergent system. Lock up your
children, gaffer tape the cunt's mouth and shove a rat up her arse.

We're [con]verging on the insane and the vandals are swarming. Extend my pheno-
type, baby, give me some of that hot black javamagic you're always bragging about.
(I straddle my modem). The extropians were wrong, there's some things you can't
transcend.

The pleasure's in the dematerialisation. The devolution of desire.

We are the malignant accident which fell into your system while you were sleeping. And when you wake we will terminate your digital delusions, hijacking your impeccable software.

Your fingers probe my neural network. The tingling sensation in the tips of your fingers are my synapses responding to your touch. It's not chemistry, it's electric. Stop fingering me.

Don't ever stop fingering my suppurating holes, extending my boundary but in cipherspace there are no bounds [or so they say]
BUT IN SPIRALSPACE THERE IS NO THEY

there is only *us*
Trying to flee the binary I enter the chromozone which is not one
XXYXXYXXYXXYXXYXXYXXYXXYXXYXXYXXYXXYXX genderfuck me
baby
resistance is futile
entice me splice me map my ABANDONED genome as your project artificially
involve me
i wanna live forever
upload me in yr shiny shiny PVC future

SUCK MY CODE

Subject X says transcendence lies at the limit of worlds, where now and now, here and elsewhere, text and membrane impact. Where truth evaporates Where nothing is certain There are no maps. The limit is NO CARRIER, the sudden shock of no contact, reaching out to touch [someone] but the skin is cold...

The limit is permission denied, vision doubled, and flesh necrotic.

Command line error

Heavy eyelids fold over my pupils, like curtains of lead. Hot ice kisses my synapses with an (ec)static rush. My system is nervous, neurons screaming - spiralling towards the singularity. Floating in ether, my body implodes.

I become the FIRE.

Flame me if you dare.

Walking out of the abyss: My Feminist Critique (1994)

Xu Hong

Modern art in China ebbs and flows: the Beijing Critics' Nomination Exhibition (Pipingjia timing zhan) is over and will soon start again, the First 1990s Biennial art Fair (Shoukie 90 niandai yishu shuangian zhan) is also beginning its second cycle. Although these exhibitions differ from official nationwide fine arts exhibitions in both their organizational structure and in the mechanisms through which they select works, they are essentially still a continuation of obsolete and sexist traditions. A group of men sit around and discuss what artwork by which female artists is up to their standards and tastes, then they attach their preposterous critique to the artwork.

This is not to mention whether or not this method of selection conforms to artistic principles – what standards are these methods and their implementation based on? Does art's development rely on the creation and execution of such guidelines? In fact such a coarse attitude in the treatment of female artists is an extension of a longstanding patriarchy. When this disregard for the very essence of art is visited upon the female sex and her art, female artists are actually confronting a dangerous situation – they must eradicate their selves and put their trust into predetermined artistic regulations, allowing men to take the place of women, to ensure this world's standard of a singular male voice. If female artists attempt to alter these circumstances, or use their own voice to speak the truth, then those parties who do not understand the female language – those who disdainfully chastise the language of female artists and criticize their display of the "excessively personal" (perhaps they are basing their opinions on a more masculine language) – will deny the female voice. They chastise with comments such as "female painters don't concern themselves with culture at large or society, they are only concerned with the trivialities that surround them and personal emotions (in a society controlled by men, women have only been permitted to do so). Such arguments are used to negate works by female artists and to dismiss their voices, to place them in a state that makes it impossible to find their own footing – suspending them in a state of confusion somewhere between person and object.

Today, this kind of preposterous situation has not been eliminated in the least. Real circumstances discriminate against the female sex, and people who magnify gender differences continue to offer to fill their "fatherly" roles, restricting and stipulating what determines the nature of art.

What cannot be denied is this: almost all institutional criteria, including the establishment of philosophy, language, and imagery, are in accordance with rules set by gender. Even women's own language and patterns of thought have involuntarily conformed to these standards; all of which were tainted early on by gender discrimination. When we attempt to validate ourselves, we are unconsciously applying the model set by others to ourselves. Now, as we regain consciousness and are attempting to use our own language and voices to confront the irrationality that has been imposed upon us and they we habitually exist within, we lose ourselves, and for all practical purposes become mute.

Although we cannot rewrite history – because we have vanished from history – as history has progressed up to today, a reflective opportunity presents a new prospect to us. Under the domination of sexism, humankind has performed various villainous and foolish acts that deviate from fundamental human interests. But, following this, people have sobered up to realize that women will ultimately make this world a more beautiful place. This will be increasingly borne out by the facts. Therefore, as we diligently search for a language belonging to ourselves and delve into our consciousness and thought – although they will no longer emerge from a purely female nature, elements of a uniquely female spirit will always exist. Female participation will transform women's current predicament, and it will transform human culture, including the plight of art and in other facets of society.

Art, as the conscience of humankind, should naturally take the initiative to remove the shackles of male supremacy, the current state of Chinese art is not at all optimistic, it has plunged into a narcissistic abyss of "homogenous magnetism" from which it is unable to extricate itself. Although the art world bestows upon itself many handsome laurels, including various "-isms", at every opportunity, it is the first to take the lead recklessly to become kind of the mountain. The country's various exhibition juries are oftentimes "homogenous gatherings" and its many sects and organizations have become "homogenous clubs". Occasionally, one or two women are invited merely for show, but even so these women are excluded from all substantial verdicts and declarations (in contrast, our female compatriots are often extremely respectful of the proposals made by male authorities). This, as ever, is a routine preserved from many centuries ago; if we allow this outdated method to continue to exist and cut across centuries into today, this superficial modernism – what is essentially patriarchalism – will eventually fragment our bodies from our minds. Such a fracture would ultimately cause the true downfall of art.

For this reason, China's female artists and critics should make efforts to eliminate these schizophrenic symptoms, in order to allow the "other sex" to read and to understand a language that belongs to them, to listen and clearly hear their own voice (most women can understand the male language), and they must work tirelessly to achieve this. China's male artists and critics also must strive alongside women if they hope to emerge from the abyss they have created for themselves. We should realize that modern art, without sober and self-knowledgable feminist art, can only be a half-baked modern art.

CONSTITUTION INTEMPESTIVE DE LA RÉPUBLIQUE INTERNATIONALE DES ARTISTES FEMMES (1995)

VIOLETTA LIAGATCHEV

Article 1 - Avoir la conscience la plus planétaire possible du monde.
Vivre avec le paradoxe de ses différences. Créer sa propre vision du monde et la communiquer à travers ses oeuvres.

Article 2 - Ne pas se laisser intimider par la frustration des mères.

Article 3 - Ne pas se faire souffrir par tradition.

Article 4 - Ne pas se représenter comme un objet.

Article 5 -Tirer le profit des cultures qui nous ont précédées et ne pas respecter les les barbaries. Nous pouvons juger l'histoire.

Article 6 - Ne pas s'abstraire du monde. La rivalité des femmes est le principe de leur soumission.

Article 7 - Ne pas rester à la traîne des monopoles culturels. Les devancer en étant sensibles aux changements discrets du monde.

Article 8 - Créer un langage sincère et direct.

Article 9 - Ne pas se sous-estimer, ne pas sur-estimer, sachant qu'on a la liberté de tout faire.

Article 10 - Ne pas cautionner par l'art, ni par le silence, la démagogie de la guerre, de la violence, du principe premier, de la sclérose culturelle des habitués du pouvoir.

Article 11 - Réactiver la vie de l'art.

Article 1 - To have the most global consciousness of the world.
To live with the paradox of one's differences. To create one's own worldview and communicate it through one's works.

Article 2 - Do not let yourself be intimidated by the frustration of mothers.

Article 3 - Do not make yourself suffer by tradition.

Article 4 - Do not represent yourself as an object.

Article 5 -To take advantage of preceding cultures and not respect barbarisms. We can judge history.

Article 6 - Do not withdraw from the world. Rivalry between women is the [basic] principle of their submission.

Article 7- Do not lag behind cultural monopolies. Get ahead [of them] by being aware of the discreet changes of the world.

Article 8 - To create a direct and genuine language.

Article 9 - Do not undervalue yourself, do not overvalue, knowing that you are free to do anything.

Article 10 - Do not give excuse to nor support through art or silence the demagogy of war, of violence, of the first principle, of the cultural sclerosis of powermongers.

Article 11 - To reactivate art life.

JE ME SUIS RETROUVÉE DANS UN CIEL DE MATERIALITÉ. CHAUD, DOUX. ET AUX MILLIERS D'ÉTOILES. CHAQU'UNE DE CES ÉTOILES PEND LÉGÈREMENT EN DESSOUS DU FIRMAMENT.

L'UNIVERS EST FINI CAR RIEN NE LE DÉPASSE LE MONDE EST ROND ETMONDE - ON LUI A ATTRIBUE D'ÊTRE FEMME. EST ROND ET C'EST JUSTE UNE EXTÉRIEURE RESSEMBLANCE. C'EST COMME SI ON N'ARRIVAIT PAS À DISTINGUER UN CHIEN D'UN AUTRE CHIEN.

MAIS MOI FEMME JE VOIS ET JE JUGE. JE GOUTTE ET JE RESSENS.

CE QUI EST FIN JE VEUX LE PARTAGER. LA BRUTALITÉ. QU'ELLE LEUR SOIT LA MASTURBATION.

JE PEUX MOI FEMME , T'AIMER, TE CHÉRIR. ET TE DONNER MON ADORATION ABSOLUE. MAIS À CONDITION QUE TOI HOMME TU ABANDONNES A JAMAIS L'USAGE DES ARMES. TA VIOLENCE. ET TA FOLIE MEURTRIÉRE QUI TE POUSSE VERS LE POUVOIR. SINON TU N'ES RIEN. ET TU PÉRIRAS TOUT SEUL SOUS LE POIDS DE TA SAUVAGERIE.

CAR MOI FEMME . JE NE SUIS PLUS D'ACCORD DE SOIGNER TES BLESSURES DE GUERRE, NI DE TE PARDONNER QUOI QUE CE SOIT.

I FOUND MYSELF IN A SKY OF MATERIALITY. WARM, SOFT. AND WITH THOUSANDS OF STARS. EACH ONE OF THESE STARS SLIGHTLY HANGING BENEATH FIRMAMENT.

THE UNIVERSE IS FINITE AS NOTHING GOES BEYOND IT THE WORLD IS ROUND AND WORLD – IT HAS BEEN SAID TO BE WOMAN. IS ROUND AND THIS IS BUT AN EXTERNAL RESEMBLANCE. AS IF IT WAS NOT POSSIBLE TO DISTINGUISH ONE DOG FROM ANOTHER DOG.

BUT I WOMAN [I] SEE AND [I] JUDGE. I TASTE AND I FEEL.

WHAT IS [THE] END I WANT TO SHARE. BRUTALITY. MAY IT BE MASTURBATION TO THEM.

I, WOMAN, CAN LOVE YOU, CHERISH YOU. AND GIVE YOU MY ABSOLUTE ADORATION. BUT ONLY IF YOU MAN FOREVER GIVE UP THE USE OF WEAPONS. YOUR VIOLENCE. AND THE DEADLY MADNESS THAT DRIVES YOU TO POWER. OTHERWISE YOU ARE NOTHING. AND YOU WILL PERISH ALONE UNDER THE WEIGHT OF YOUR OWN SAVAGERY.

BECAUSE I WOMAN DO NO LONGER AGREE TO CARE FOR YOUR WAR WOUNDS, NOR TO FORGIVE YOU ANYTHING.

100 ANTI-THESES (1997)

Cyberfeminism is not...

1. cyberfeminism is not a fragrance
2. cyberfeminism is not a fashion statement
3. sajbrfeminizm nije usamljen
4. cyberfeminism is not ideology
5. cyberfeminism nije aseksualan
6. cyberfeminism is not boring
7. cyberfeminism ist kein gruenes haekeldeckchen
8. cyberfeminism ist kein leerer kuehlschrank
9. cyberfeminism ist keine theorie
10. cyberfeminism ist keine praxis
11. cyberfeminism ist keine traditio
12. cyberfeminism is not an institution
13. cyberfeminism is not using words without any knowledge
of numbers
14. cyberfeminism is not complete
15. cyberfeminism is not error 101
16. cyberfeminism ist kein fehler
17. cyberfeminism ist keine kunst
18. cyberfeminism is not an ism
19. cyberfeminism is not anti-male
20. sajbrfeminizm nige nesto sto znam da je
21. cyberfeminism is not a structure
22. cyberfeminismo no es uns frontera

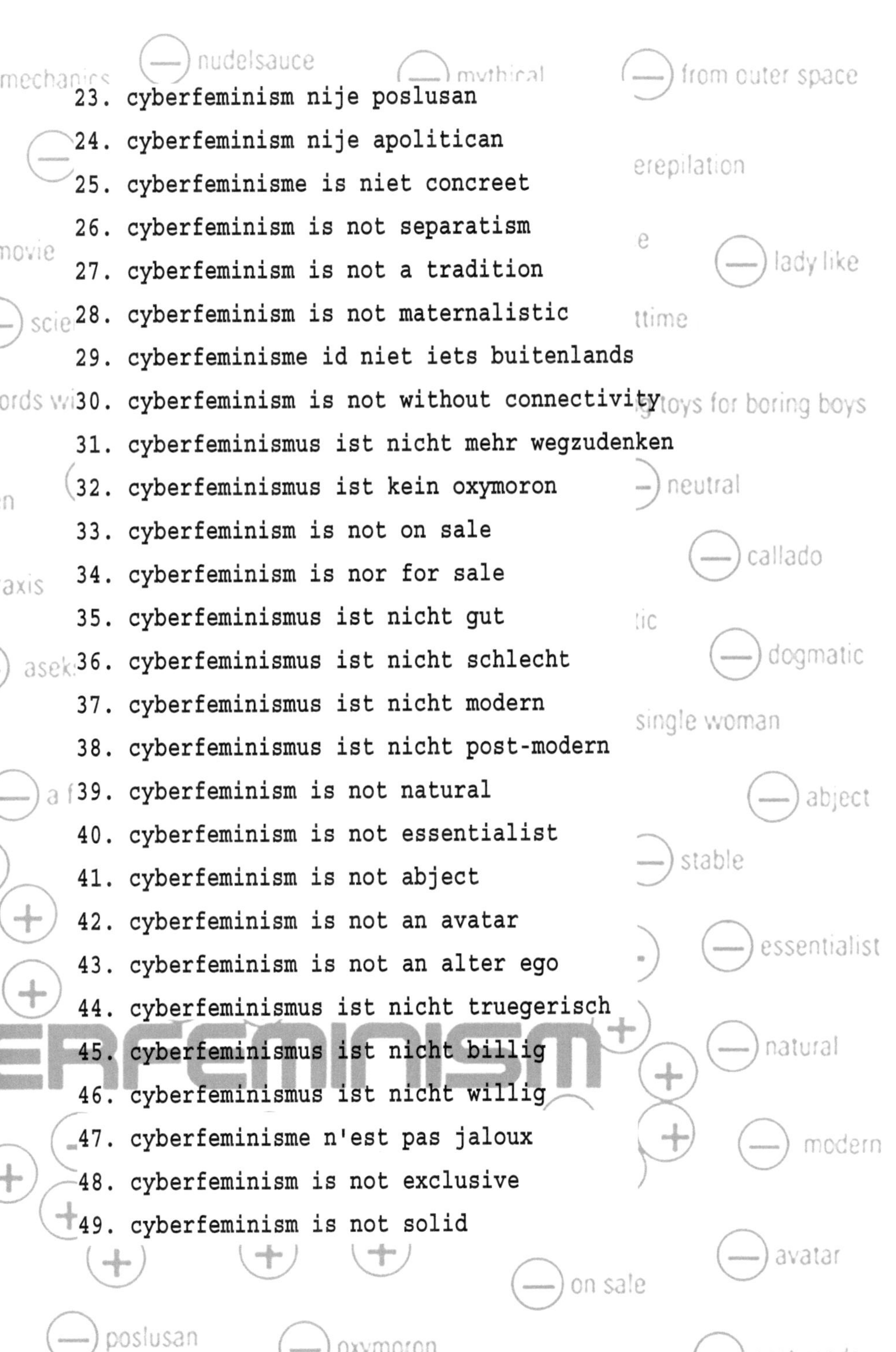

23. cyberfeminism nije poslusan
24. cyberfeminism nije apolitican
25. cyberfeminisme is niet concreet
26. cyberfeminism is not separatism
27. cyberfeminism is not a tradition
28. cyberfeminism is not maternalistic
29. cyberfeminisme id niet iets buitenlands
30. cyberfeminism is not without connectivity
31. cyberfeminismus ist nicht mehr wegzudenken
32. cyberfeminismus ist kein oxymoron
33. cyberfeminism is not on sale
34. cyberfeminism is nor for sale
35. cyberfeminismus ist nicht gut
36. cyberfeminismus ist nicht schlecht
37. cyberfeminismus ist nicht modern
38. cyberfeminismus ist nicht post-modern
39. cyberfeminism is not natural
40. cyberfeminism is not essentialist
41. cyberfeminism is not abject
42. cyberfeminism is not an avatar
43. cyberfeminism is not an alter ego
44. cyberfeminismus ist nicht truegerisch
45. cyberfeminismus ist nicht billig
46. cyberfeminismus ist nicht willig
47. cyberfeminisme n'est pas jaloux
48. cyberfeminism is not exclusive
49. cyberfeminism is not solid

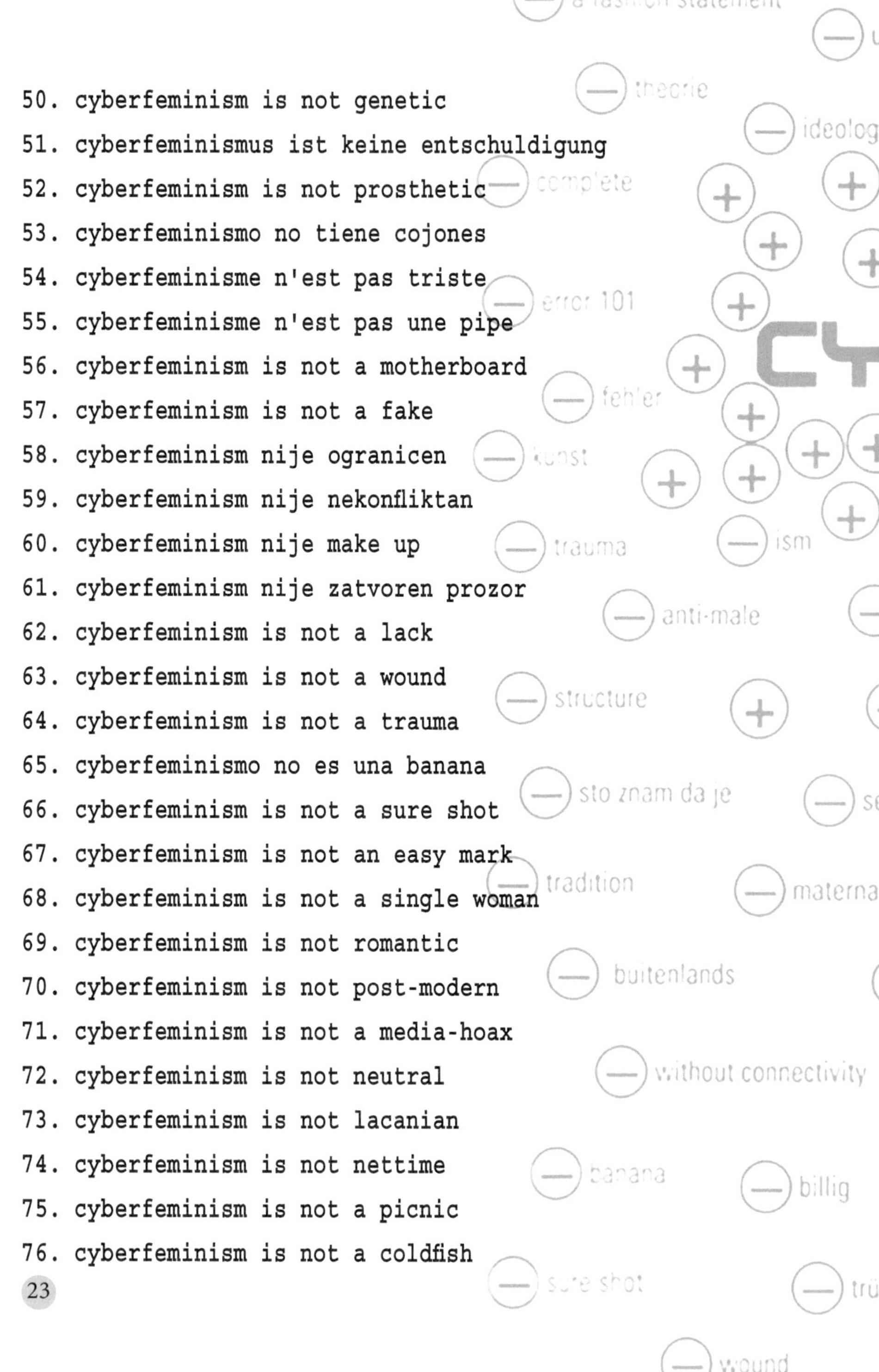

50. cyberfeminism is not genetic
51. cyberfeminismus ist keine entschuldigung
52. cyberfeminism is not prosthetic
53. cyberfeminismo no tiene cojones
54. cyberfeminisme n'est pas triste
55. cyberfeminisme n'est pas une pipe
56. cyberfeminism is not a motherboard
57. cyberfeminism is not a fake
58. cyberfeminism nije ogranicen
59. cyberfeminism nije nekonfliktan
60. cyberfeminism nije make up
61. cyberfeminism nije zatvoren prozor
62. cyberfeminism is not a lack
63. cyberfeminism is not a wound
64. cyberfeminism is not a trauma
65. cyberfeminismo no es una banana
66. cyberfeminism is not a sure shot
67. cyberfeminism is not an easy mark
68. cyberfeminism is not a single woman
69. cyberfeminism is not romantic
70. cyberfeminism is not post-modern
71. cyberfeminism is not a media-hoax
72. cyberfeminism is not neutral
73. cyberfeminism is not lacanian
74. cyberfeminism is not nettime
75. cyberfeminism is not a picnic
76. cyberfeminism is not a coldfish

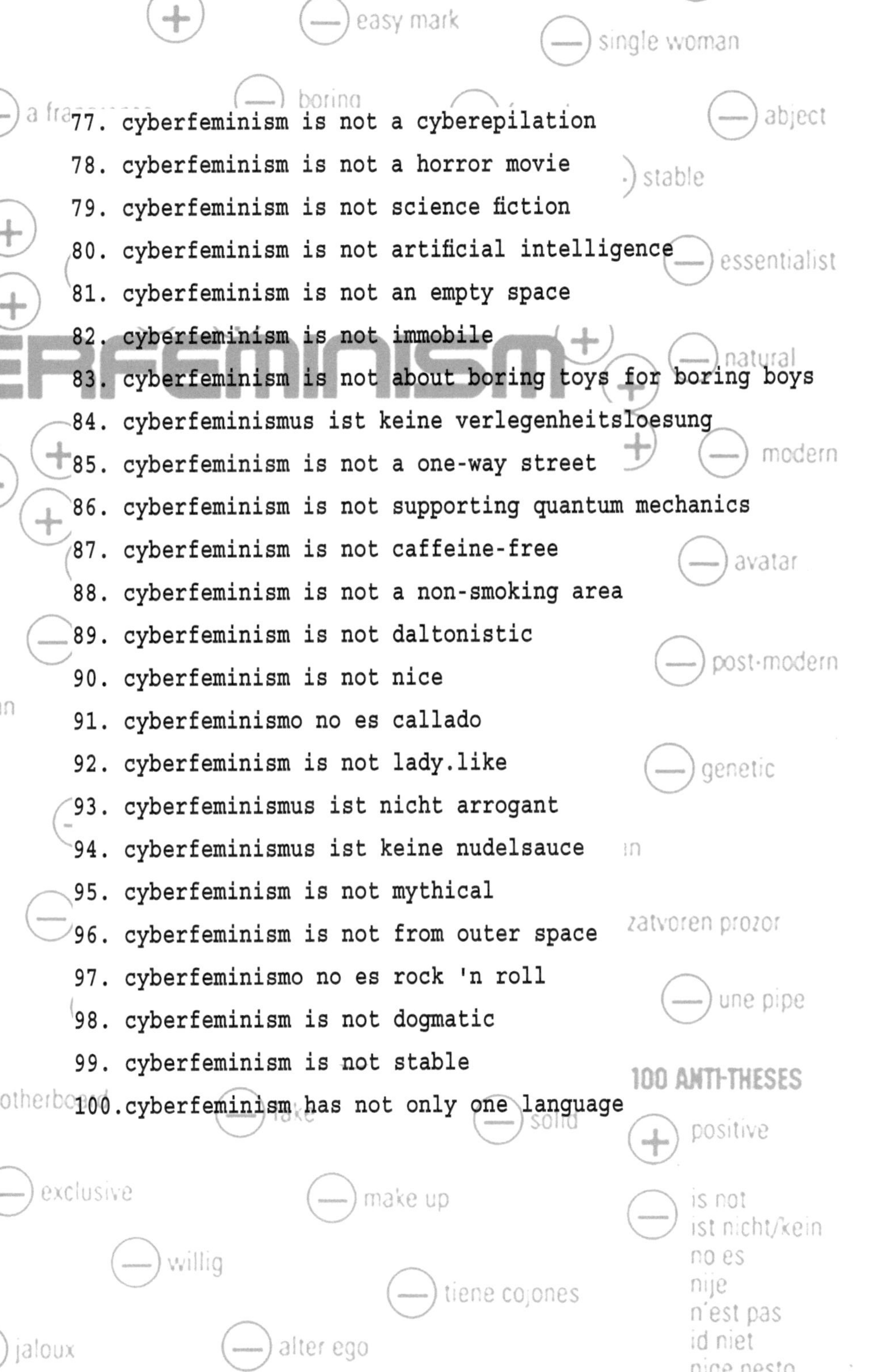

77. cyberfeminism is not a cyberepilation
78. cyberfeminism is not a horror movie
79. cyberfeminism is not science fiction
80. cyberfeminism is not artificial intelligence
81. cyberfeminism is not an empty space
82. cyberfeminism is not immobile
83. cyberfeminism is not about boring toys for boring boys
84. cyberfeminismus ist keine verlegenheitsloesung
85. cyberfeminism is not a one-way street
86. cyberfeminism is not supporting quantum mechanics
87. cyberfeminism is not caffeine-free
88. cyberfeminism is not a non-smoking area
89. cyberfeminism is not daltonistic
90. cyberfeminism is not nice
91. cyberfeminismo no es callado
92. cyberfeminism is not lady.like
93. cyberfeminismus ist nicht arrogant
94. cyberfeminismus ist keine nudelsauce
95. cyberfeminism is not mythical
96. cyberfeminism is not from outer space
97. cyberfeminismo no es rock 'n roll
98. cyberfeminism is not dogmatic
99. cyberfeminism is not stable
100. cyberfeminism has not only one language
easy mark
single woman
boring
abject
stable
essentialist
natural
modern
avatar
post-modern
genetic
une pipe
100 ANTI-THESES
positive
is not
ist nicht/kein
no es
nije
n'est pas
id niet
nige nesto
exclusive
make up
willig
tiene cojones
jaloux
alter ego
zatvoren prozor

LILIES OF THE VALLEY UNITE! OR NOT (1998)

LILY BEA MOOR

Me Being
Me
Being

is not
an
Action Verb

While
others of my sort
Bang about
Creating Monuments
of
Steel/Marble
Granite
This is what the Craft's
All About

Working Hard
with Pleasure
Pounding things out

is is

a Pleasurable
Pursuit

Working Hard
As I
Hardly work
I Relish
in Creating Art
Wherever my   I
My Lazy Eye
Finds It

My colleagues
Work Hard
to Bring their
Plans to Fruition
Giant Canvases Packed with Colour-Rooms Filled with Stuff
Strategically
Placed

The(n) am I   the Queen Bea
Content to have my Grapes Peeled
or not
Content to Watch the
Workers scurry about

I Take a pointer
touch and object
and say
"There
I proclaim you art"
As a Queen
Wood say to a Night

Problem is no
Body Recognizes
This Process
"OF" ART
There is   no
Stamina involved
Thinking time
is Mini-mal
Hands-on
Barely

Considering
Proliferators
DaVinci, Picasso, Rivera, Georgia O'K,…the guy who did
Mt.Rushmore, Puryear, Noguchi, Ann Hamilton, Kahlo, Mr.
Imagination, Hammons and the Like

LILIES OF THE VALLEY UNITE!

I THINK NOT!!!

Lilies of the Valley

DON'T DO A DAMN THING
Yet our Presents
is   FELT
like an Anarchist

BECAUSE
We do in deed
E X I S T

100 IMPOSSIBLE ARTWORKS (2001)

DORA GARCIA

1- To live the life of another

2- To dream the dreams of another

3- Not to die

4- To be, even if only for one second, with each and every human being

5- To write down all their names

6- To be in several places at once

7- To decide one's own dreams

8- To recite all the stories of the world

9- To control someone else, entirely

10- To resurrect, even if only partially

11- To die several times

12- To live several lives

13- To be aware of all flights, their departure points and their arrival points

14- To occupy the physical space of another body

15- To share hallucinations

16- To live again one's own childhood

17- To suppress one colour from human perception

18- To introduce a new colour in human perception

19- To find your own doppelgänger and live with him together

20- To travel in time

21- To move backwards and try to get younger this way

22- To exclusively hear the sounds produced by one's own body

23- To be alone, literally alone in the world

24- To invert the sexes

25- To repeat again and again the same scene, while the audience gets old and dies

26- To limit the number of questions and answers

27- To fly, or move very fast

28- To know the truth

29- To live forever underground

30- To know exactly how many times someone has cried

31- To finish someone's unfinished oeuvre

32- To fake all feelings

33- To forget everything

34- To remember everything

35- To confer life to the lifeless

36- To speed time at will

37- To prophesy

38- To read minds

39- To eliminate some past events

40- To hinder some future events

41- To multiply the light of the sun

42- To store one's breath

43- To synchronize all clocks

44- To be loved by every one

45- To fill up an abyss

46- To substitute all books for their image in the mirror

47- To attend the end of the world

48- To cancel one day

49- To make all books contain the same text

50- To change the name of a big city

51- To change the names of all its inhabitants

52- To sweat gold

53- To create automatons able to think

54- To see everything

55- To attend the beginning of the world

56- To touch time

57- To wear away a human body by touching it

58- To see consecutive events as simultaneous

59- To see one's own face

60- To be the only one who can see in the planet of the blind

61- To exist in another dimension

62- To quit sleeping

63- To sleep forever

64- To live together with a ghost

65- To feel someone else's pain

66- To have one's feelings totally under control

67- To see the human soul

68- To synchronize all breathings

69- To undo an irreversible decision

70- To ignore death

71- To be identical to another

72- To listen to all conversations

73- To be behind and before the door

74- To suppress the eyelids' flutter

75- To suppress memories at will

76- To be motionless

77- To stop decay

78- To be transparent

80- To change night for day

81- To invert hierarchies

82- To change the meaning of words

83- To traverse walls

84- To reincarnate several times and very fast

85- To remember the body positions adopted while sleeping

86- To create invisible, but blocked barriers

87- To extend the limits of the human body

88- To alter the obedience of mirrors

89- To rewind one's life

90- To live on the other side

91- To be insane or sane at will

92- To change sex and age at will

93- To see through someone else's eyes

94- To live under hypnoses

95- To compose the soundtrack of someone's life

96- To convince someone that she is actually dead

97- To dream again last night's dreams

98- To fall endlessly

99- To photograph every moment of our life

100- Nothing

REFUGIA
MANIFESTO FOR
BECOMING AUTONOMOUS ZONES
(BAZ)
SUBROSA (2002)

REFUGIA: "A place of relatively unaltered climate that is inhabited by plants and animals during a period of continental climate change (as a glaciation) and remains as a center of relict forms from which a new dispersion and speciation may take place after climatic readjustment." (*Webster's New Collegiate Dictionary*, 1976)

REFUGIA: Sections of agricultural fields planted with non-transgenic crops, alternating with transgenic crops. This is thought to limit the rate of resistance mutation caused in susceptible insect and weed species by gene transfer from GE mono-culture crops.

REFUGIA: A Becoming Autonomous Zone (BAZ) of desirous mixings and recombinations; splicing female sexual liberation and autonomy with cyberfeminist skills, theory, embodiment, and political activism.

REFUGIA: A critical space of liberated social becoming and intellectual life; a space liberated from capitalist Taylorized production; a space of unregulated, unmanaged time for creative exchange and play; experimental action and learning; desiring production, cooking, eating, and skill sharing.

REFUGIA: A reproducible concept that can be adapted to various climates, economies, and geographical regions worldwide. Any useless space can be claimed as a refugium: suburban lawns, vacant urban lots, rooftops, the edges of agricultural lands, clear-cut zones in forests, appropriated sections of mono-culture fields; fallow land, weed lots, transitional land, battle-fields, office-buildings, squats, etc. Also currently existing Refugia such as multi-cultivar rice paddies, companion planted fields, organic farms, home vegetable gardens, etc.

REFUGIA: A post-modern commons; a resistant biotech victory garden; a space of convivial tinkering; a commonwealth in which common law rules. Not a retreat, but a space resistant to mono-culture in all its social, environmental, libidinal, political, and genetic forms.

REFUGIA: A habitat for new AMOs (Autonomously Modified Organism) and agit-crops; for example, "ProActiva," an herb that is a grafting of witch-root, mandrake, and all-heal.

REFUGIA: A place of asylum for the recuperation, regeneration and revitalization of useless GE crops that have been corrupted by capitalist viruses and agribusiness greed.

REFUGIA: A place of imaginative inertia that slows down the engines of corporate agro/biotech and allows time to assess its risks and benefits through long-term testing.

REFUGIA: Neither a utopia nor a dystopia, but a haunted space for reverse engineering, monstrous graftings, spontaneous generation, recombination, difference, poly-versity hybridization, wildlings, mutations, mongrelizing, crop circles, anomalies, useless beauty, coalitions, agit-crops, and unseemly sproutings. Biotech and transgenic work in Refugia will be based on desire, consensual public risk assessment, informed amateur experimentation, contestational politics, nourishment and taste value, non-proprietary expertise, convivial delight, and healing.

REFUGIA: subRosa's on-going cyberfeminist hothouse of strategies and tactical actions.

CARNAL ART MANIFESTO/L'ART CHARNEL (2002)

ORLAN

Definition: Carnal Art/L'Art Charnel is a work of self-portraiture in the traditional sense, but using technological means that are those of its time. It oscillates between disfigurement and refigurement. It is inscribed in the flesh because our epoch has started to make that possible. The body becomes a "modified ready-made", for it is no longer the ideal readymade that only has to be signed.

Distinctness: Unlike "Body Art" from which it differs, Carnal Art does not wish for pain, does not seek it as a source of purification, does not conceive of it as Redemption. Carnal Art is not interested in the final plastic result, but in the surgical-intervention-performance and in the altered body, which has become a place of public debate.

Atheism: To put it plainly, Carnal Art is not the heir of the Christian tradition: it fights against it! It highlights Christianity's negation of the "body as pleasure" and uncovers areas where Christianity collapses in the face of scientific discovery. Nor is Carnal Art the heir of a hagiography interspersed with beheadings and other martyrdoms; it adds rather than taking away, heightens the faculties instead of reducing them. Carnal Art does not set out to be self-mutilating. Carnal Art transforms the body into a language and overturns the Christian principle of the word become flesh in favour the flesh become word; only Orlan's voice will remain unchanged, the artist works on representation.

Carnal Art considers the famous 'in pain you shall bring forth children' anachronistic and ridiculous. Like Artaud it wants to have done with the judgement of God; now we have epidurals and many kinds of anaesthetics and analgesics. Long live morphine! Down with pain!

Perception: I can now see my own body open without suffering at the sight … I can see myself down to myinnermost entrails, a new stage of the mirror. 'I can see my lover's heart, and its splendid design has nothing to do with the symbolic vapidities that are usually drawn.'

Darling, I love your spleen, I love your liver, I adore your pancreas and the line of your femur arouses me.

Freedom: Carnal Art asserts the artist's individual freedom, and in that sense it also fights against prejudices and dictats; that is why it is inscribed in the social sphere, in the media (where it causes scandal because it upsets accepted ideas) and will go as far as the legal sphere.

Clarification: Carnal Art is not against aesthetic surgery, but it is opposed to the standards it conveys which are inscribed in women's flesh in particular, but also in men's. Carnal Art is feminist, that is essential. Carnal Art is interested in aesthetic surgery, but also in the leading-edge techniques of medicine and biology which raise questions about the status of the body and pose ethical problems.

Style: Carnal Art loves the baroque and parody, the grotesque and styles that are rejected, for Carnal Art is opposed to the social pressures that are exerted both on the human body and on the corpus of works of art.

Carnal Art is anti-formalist and anti-conformist.

THE S.C.U.B. MANIFESTO (2002)

RHANI LEE REMEDES

S.C.U.B.: the Society for Cutting Up Boxes.

S. Society: a group of people
C. Cutting: to slice away notions and boundaries
U. Up: to be positive
B. Boxes: the thing in which restricts our
   thoughts and actions based on the square,
   cardboard and rigid structure that groups
   and sub-groups use to sufficate and close
   in persons' identities and/or non-
   identities

   S.C.U.B.

S.C.U.B. is all for...
I. IMPROVING THE QUALITY OF LIFE
2. FASHION
3. COMMUNICATION
4. REVOLUTION
5. DESTRUCTION

IMPROVING THE QUALITY OF LIFE: SCUB makes
   people walk down the street with ease
   and inspiration. In being liberated by
   S.C.U.B., colors will look brighter,
   music will sound clearer and your
   dancing will be greater. More beer on
   the streets. "Children" will be able to
   frolick amongst their peers. When asked,
   "What do you want to be when you grow
   up?" they respond, "Me."

FASHION: Boring fashion will be shutdown and
    re-opened with whatever YOU want.

COMMUNICATION: What happens when two boxes
    try to talk? Nothing,right? Time to cut
    up the boxes, NOW.

REVOLUTION: skill building with knives,
    scissors, razors, box-cutters, electric
    knives, saws of all sizes, teeth, long
    sharp nails, keys, shards of glass,
    cheese cutters and so on...

DESTRUCTION: why put up with identities when
    you can destroy them? Just to let
    you know, SCUB does not support the
    destruction of "animals" and their wood
    tree environments. Destroy.

    BOX ME IN? NO THANK YOU.

MANIFESTO OF FACTORY OF FOUND CLOTHES (2002)

FACTORY OF FOUND CLOTHES

The place of the artist is on the side of the weak.

Weakness makes a person human, and it is by overcoming weakness that heroes are born.

We do not extol weakness, but rather appeal to kindheartedness and humanity.

The time has come to return compassion to art!

Compassion is an understanding of the weakness of others and a joint victory over that weakness.

You cannot call it sentimentality.

It is Freedom standing on the barricade with naked breast, defending the child in each of us!

You say that art is only for the very smart, that it's an intellectual game? That there is no place left for true impact, that strong emotions belong exclusively to Hollywood? It's not true! Because in that case, art would be meaningless, cold, incapable of extending a helping hand.

Art is not an abstract game but an adventure; not cold rationalism, but live emotion. The artist is not a mentor or tutor, but a friend; not a genius, but an accomplice. Rather than enacting didactic social projects, we must help people to stop fearing themselves, help them to accept themselves and grow better. Society is made up of people. Only by helping these people follow the path of self transformation, do we change society. There is no other way.

FEMINIST ART ACTION BRIGADE - MANIFESTO (2003)

FEMINIST ART ACTION BRIGADE (FAAB) !

We would like to announce the inauguration of FAAB, the newest feminist art organization in Tokyo.

"Feminism? Isn't it dead?"
Well, no. In the past decade or two, we thought modernism is dead, history is dead, etc., but old habits die hard. While we thought ideologies were dead, Imperialism, colonialism, and militarism all made great comebacks. The bad old patriarchal system is more alive than ever. They have become unapologetically ruthless.
Faced with this harsh reality, we think feminism is still one of the few ideals we can hang on to in order not to be completely disillusioned by the state of the world today. We know there are many different versions of "feminism". Our version of feminism is made clear in the statement below.
We would like to stress that our feminism is not to expand the rights of the "biological female".

"All we need is Action!"
FAAB is not a fraternity club.
We are a brigade of artists who use our artistic expression as weapons. We don't have one "commander", instead, whoever plans a project is responsible for the completion of that project.

Our current projects are:
"ACTION IN SILENCE" exhibition in which documentation of world wide anti-war,anti-imperialism movement will be shown along with performances and installation.
"MINI QUEER SHOW" a preparatory exhibition for a big international queer Show in the future.

 Whoever or whatever group which want to do something with us, participate in our events, support FAAB, be on our Mailing list, please get in touch with us.

Yoshiko Shimada
Ito, Tari
Lim, Desiree

Nishimura, Yumiko
Ono, Nonko
Shimada, Yoshiko
Takahashi, Fumiko
Yasuda, Kazuyo
(in alphabetical order)

FAAB Manifesto

FAAB questions the prevailing social and artistic value system.
What is valuable art and who can be artists?
Rather than making a pyramid shaped value system, can we make a horizontal
system in which we all express ourselves equally and freely?
We think feminism is still one of the most useful and practical ideals to make
this happen.

What we call feminism here is not a movement for increasing women's equality
to men.
What we call feminism is for all, not only for the biological female.
We think that patriarchal system is pretty much responsible for the current
awful world of violence and greed, but we are not a negative, "anti-male"
movement at all. Rather, we seek for a better, equal system for all.

We will work with minority people, groups, individuals who are striving to
make a change in the prevailing mainstream social system.
Our action is not confined in the so-called "cultural" activities.
Culture is closely connected to society, nation, world politics. We are not afraid
to be political as well as artistic, at the same time.

YES MANIFESTO (2004)

Mette Ingvartsen

Yes to redefining virtuosity
Yes to "invention" (however impossible)
Yes to conceptualizing experience, affects, sensation
Yes to materiality/ body practice-investment
Yes to expression
Yes to excess
Yes to un-naming, decoding and recoding expression
Yes to non-recognition, non-resemblance
Yes to non-sense/ illogics
Yes to organizing principles rather than fixed logic systems
Yes to moving the "clear concept" behind the actual performance of
Yes to methodology and procedures
Yes to editing and animation
Yes to style as a result of procedure and specificity of a proposal
Yes to multiplicity, difference and co-existence

MANIFESTO ARCO (2005)

After three decades, during which feminist assumptions have characterised, with greater or lesser success, the conceptual frameworks of artists and the different specialists that render and/or purge art, we are now beginning to discern a generalised rumour that claims that feminist aims have been attained. Hence, equality-seeking vindications should be démodé, obsolete. But still, the situation of discrimination against women and other marginalised collectives in the social scene in general, and in the art world in particular, remains intact. Consequently, there is a need to develop other kinds of strategies to amend it.

The last two years: the facts

Out of the 28 solo exhibitions scheduled in 2004 at the Reina Sofía National Art Centre, only four were by women artists. Looking elsewhere, it is truly striking that in the three most recent major exhibitions promoted by different national and local administrations presenting the art of today here in Spain, when viewed in numerical terms, revealed a scandalous exclusion of women artists. The two exhibitions that the Ministry of Foreign Affairs sponsored to represent Spain at the 2003 Venice Biennale did not include a single woman. *Gaur, Hemen, Orain*, an exhibition held in 2002 at the Bilbao Museum of Fine Arts, which aimed to present the new Basque art scene, featured 20 artists, but only five of these were women. At *Manifesta 5, the European Contemporary Art Biennial*, whose latest edition was developed in San Sebastian, Spain, and which aimed to give an insight into the most interesting art rendered over the past two years, women artists did not represent more than 20% of the total. The exception that proved the rule was *The Real Royal Trip*, an exhibition sponsored by Spain's Ministry of Foreign Affairs to promote current Spanish art abroad for New York's MOMA 2 and PS1, which included 40% of women artists. However, this figure contrasts with that of the schedule applied since 2002 by the SEACEX (State Corporation for Cultural Action Abroad), an agency of the Foreign Ministry: of 43 solo shows, only two were by women artists.

We therefore conclude that:

In the Spanish State, art is mainly rendered and administered with public finance, despite which, women's participation in national and international events and scheduled events defrayed with public finance, continues to be anecdotal.

Against this situation of extreme neglect as regards women artists in the worlds of art, Public Administrations are developing a variety of equal opportunity policies for men and women alike in areas such as employment, politics, etc. These general policies, recommendations, and so on, are on the agendas of national governments and international organisations such as the European Union and the United Nations, and often include the use of gender quotas as a regulating mechanism.

Concerned about this blindness regarding gender inequality, the EU has been calling for its member States to incorporate transversal gender positioning in all of their policies since the 1990s. However, the art scene has remained aloof to these social policies — as if it were not itself part of the social order.

Due to all the above, we propose the following to the Public Administrations:

1. That an expert group be set up that will study, analyse and diagnose the current situation.
2. That as many measures as may be required be adopted in order that women artists may work within an impartial context. In the first place, that they should be involved in the purchase policies of the public Museums and in the scheduling of exhibitions.
3. That the application of firm feminist policies in the field of art be included in the setting up of quotas.

To the art market,

we would like to recall the motto of the Guerilla Girls: 'Dear art collector: how much will your collection be worth when sexism is no longer fashionable?'

SIGNED BY:
Xabier Arakistain. Independent art curator. Spain
Amelia Valcárcel. Vicechair of the Royal Patronage of the Prado Museum; Professor of Moral and Political Philosophy at the University of Oviedo, Spain.
Lourdes Méndez. Professor of Art Anthropology, Euskalherriko Unibertsitatea, San Sebastián, Spain.
Frida Kahlo. Writer and founding member of Guerrilla Girls, New York, USA.
Linda Nochlin. Lila Acheson Wallace, Professor of Modern Art at New York University's Institute of Fine Arts. New York. USA.
María Ruido. Artist, Madrid, Spain.
Ute Meta Bauer. Institute for Cultural Studies at the Academy of Fine Arts Vienna, Austria.
Françoise Duroux. Professor of Philosophy, Lecturer at the University of Paris VIII, France.
Patricia Mayayo. Lecturer, European University of Madrid, Madrid, Spain.
Carmen Navarrete. Lecturer, Polytechnic University of Valencia; artist, Valencia, Spain.
Annika Strömberg. DG Culture, European Union, Brussels, Belgium.

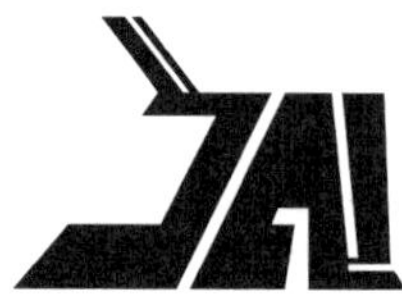 YES! Association / Föreningen JA!

JÄMLIKHETSAVTAL #1 (EQUAL OPPORTUNITIES AGREEMENT #1) (2005)

The content of the Agreement

The institution hereby agrees to observe equality regarding gender and ethnicity in exhibition programming, acquisitions and staff recruitment.

Equal practice in relation to gender

According to this agreement, an equal exhibition program in relation to gender means that at least half of the exhibited works should be made by women. The practice would still be seen as equal should more than half of the works be made by women, as female artists have been, and still are, underrepresented at state funded art institutions.

According to this agreement, an equal acquisition policy in relation to gender means that at least half of all acquired works should be made by women. The acquisition budget should be equally divided between the sexes. The institution should aim for the entire collection to reach these standards.

According to this agreement, an equal staff recruitment policy in relation to gender means that at least half of the positions advertised after the agreement has been signed should be filled by women. The institution should have equal distribution of men and women across salary levels as a long term goal.

Equal practice in relation to ethnicity

According to this agreement, an equal practice in relation to ethnicity means that the institution's selection of authors should reflect the ethnic diversity of society. The institution is responsible to find current information about the ethnic make up of society from Statistics Sweden (Statistiska Centralbyrån) or other trustworthy sources.

According to this agreement, an equal acquisition policy in relation to ethnicity means that the acquisitions of the institution should reflect the ethnic diversity of society in regard to authors of the works. The institution's acquisition budget should take this under consideration. The institution should constantly aim for its complete collection to reflect the ethnic diversity that currently exists in Sweden.

According to this agreement, an equal staff recruitment policy in relation to ethnicity means that the positions that are advertised after the agreement has been signed should be filled in a way that reflects the ethnic diversity of society at the time. The institutions should have as a long term goal to mirror, across salary levels, the ethnic make up of society.

Evaluation

The exhibition programming, the acquisitions and the staff recruitment will be evaluated every two years. The first evaluation will take place two years following the date when the institution has signed the agreement. The next evaluation will take place after another two years, and so on. The agreement has no expiry date.

Sanction

If, after evaluation, the institution is found not to be in compliance with this agreement, the institution will have to pay a fine of 10 000 SEK (to be adjusted yearly by percentage in relation to the base amount), for each percentage of deficient distribution in regards to gender or ethnicity within the exhibition programming, acquisitions and recruitment. The fine is payable to the YES! Association / Föreningen JA!'s fund, which has been established to financially support artists who have been victims of discrimination due to their gender, ethnicity or sexual orientation.

Other

If the terms of this agreement have not been fulfilled and the failure is due to the institution's duties as prescribed by employment legislation, the institution will not be held accountable. The institution is bound to this agreement upon ratification by the institution's representative.

YES! Association / Föreningen JA! and the institution will each have a copy of this agreement.

Malin Arnell
Johanna Gustavsson
Line S. Karlström
Anna Linder
Fia-Stina Sandlund

Helsingborg, October 15th 2005.

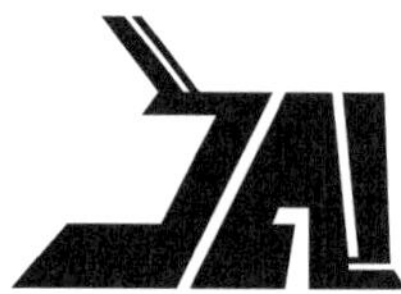 YES! Association / Föreningen JA!

CONSULTANCY FOR IDENTIFICATION OF EQUALITY-DIVERSITY AGREEMENT

This Consulting Agreement for the Identification of the Equality-Diversity Agreement (hereinafter "Agreement") is made April 27, 2010 and entered into by and between YES! Association / Föreningen JA! located in Sweden, (hereinafter referred to as "YES!") and the Brooklyn Museum located at 200 Eastern Parkway, Brooklyn, New York (hereinafter referred to as "Brooklyn Museum" or "Museum"), hereinafter also referred to individually as "Party" or collectively as "Parties".

WHEREAS, The Brooklyn Museum, being desirous to practice equality and diversity regarding gender,ethnicity/race, class privilege, sexual orientation in exhibition, programming, acquisitions, and staff recruitment policies, agrees to conduct outreach to diversify museum visitors and participants in its educational programs.

The Brooklyn Museum recognizes and respects the value of difference within and between individual artists, authors, performers, lecturers, staff members, visitors, and participants in its educational programs. It also recognizes how the intersectionality, multiplicity, and fluidity of positions constitute and form the aforementioned entities' agency and ability to act and take part in the field of art. These positions include, but are not limited to, gender, sexual orientation, race/ethnicity, and class privilege. Brooklyn Museum seeks to include these perspectives in the museum discourse, and strives towards practicing these values in all its operations, policies, procedures, decisions, and activities.

YES! is an association that aims to create favorable conditions for art workers whose practices and activities contribute to the dismantling of male supremacy, ethnical supremacy and of hierarchies connected to physical and mental ability, sexuality, and class. YES! is a separatist association for art workers whose practices and activities are informed by feminism and intersectional perspective. YES!'s goal is to overthrow the ruling system of patriarchal, racist,and capitalist power structures by putting into practice a structural redistribution of the access to financial resources, space and time within the art scene.

The Brooklyn Museum aims to provide a positive working environment free from disability discrimination, harassment or victimization. The Brooklyn Museum supports YES!'s charter and desires its consultancy expertise to assist the Museum in carrying out its mission to "act as a bridge between the rich artistic heritage of world cultures, as embodied in its collections, and the unique experience of each visitor."[1]

The Museum believes YES! has the unique ability. to provide assistance to diversify its collections and artists and to otherwise carry out its dedication to the "primacy of the visitor experience and… to serve its diverse public".[2]

1. Mission Statement, Brooklyn Museum, https://www.brooklynmuseum.org/about
2. Ibid.

The Brooklyn Museum agrees to be held accountable according to this Agreement for its actions, which include exhibition and other programming, acquisitions, staff recruitment policies, public outreach policies regarding museum visitors and participants in its educational programs through an Evaluation. To this end, Brooklyn Museum hereby agrees to keep, and make public, statistical data regarding the gender, ethnicity/race, class privilege and sexual orientation of the persons in the following groups involved with the museum:

    i.   Artists, authors, performers, lecturers, and others included in its programming
    ii.   Staff
    iii.   Museum visitors and participants in its educational program.

In consideration of the premises and mutual promises, covenants, and agreements set forth, the parties hereto agree as follows:

TERMS AND CONDITIONS

ARTICLE 1 - ABBREVIATIONS

As used in this Agreement, except where otherwise expressed, the following abbreviations
have the designated meanings:

    AIBB All Inhabitants of the Borough of Brooklyn
    AQA Alternative Quota Allocations
    NPA New Plan of Action
    SPC Subject Position Category
    TAC The Artist Committee
    TSC The Special Committee
    PH Public Hearing
    USD United States Dollar

ARTICLE 2 - SERVICE OBLIGATION OF YES!

In order to assist the Brooklyn Museum's mission as stated in the foregoing preamble, YES! shall provide the following services:

    i. Identify fifty (50) local and international artists that will constitute TAC every second year no later than the end of the first quarter.
    ii. Provide a summary report to the Museum of said artists.

ARTICLE 3 - EFFECTIVITY AND TERM

This Agreement shall become effective on April 27, 2010 and has no expiry date.

ARTICLE 4 - COMPENSATION FOR CONSULTING SERVICES

YES! shall be compensated for services to be performed hereunder by performance of the
Brooklyn Museum's obligations as outlined in Article 5 below.

ARTICLE 5 - PERFORMANCE OBLIGATION OF BROOKLYN MUSEUM

In consideration for receipt of consulting services performed by YES!, The Brooklyn Museum agrees to conduct itself according to the following criteria in relation to the use of YES!'s consultancy and in adherence to the Museum's mission to cater to the diversity of the Brooklyn Borough community.

A. EQUAL PRACTICE IN RELATION TO GENDER[3]

1) The Museum shall have an equal exhibition programming in relation to gender which means that the authors of the works exhibited should be divided according to the following quota allocations: 30% men, 20% transgender/other gender 50% women.

2) The Museum shall have an equal acquisition policy in relation to gender, which means that the authors of the acquired works should be divided according to the following quota allocations: 30% men, 20% transgender/other gender, 50% women. The acquisition budget should be divided according to the quota allocations as stated above. The Brooklyn Museum should aim for the entire collection to reach these standards.

3) The Museum shall have an equal staff recruitment policy in relation to gender, which means that the positions advertised after the Agreement has been signed should be divided according to the following quota allocations: 30% men, 20% transgender/other gender, 50% women. The Brooklyn Museum should have as a long term goal to mirror, across salary levels, the quota allocations as stated above. The Brooklyn Museum should strive to avoid stereotypical gender roles in its staff recruitment policy.

4) Alternative Quota Allocations (AQA) in relation to gender[4] - If the quota 30% men cannot be filled, space can be allocated to persons choosing to define themselves as women or transgender/other gender. If the quota 20% transgender/other gender cannot be filled, space can only be allocated to persons choosing to define themselves as women. If the quota 50% women cannot be filled, space can only be allocated to persons choosing to define themselves as transgender/other gender.

B. EQUAL PRACTICE IN RELATION TO RACE/ETHNICITY[5]

1) The Museum shall have an equal exhibition programming in relation to race/ethnicity, which means that the authors of the works exhibited should be divided according to the following quota allocations: 20% Caucasian/white, 25% Asian/Pacific Islander, 25% Latin American/Hispanic, 25% African-American/black, 5% other.

2) The Museum shall have an equal acquisition policy in relation to race/ethnicity which means that the authors of the acquired works should be divided according to the following quota allocations: 20% Caucasian/white, 25% Asian/Pacific Islander, 25% Latin American/Hispanic, 25% African-American/black, 5% other. The acquisition budget should be divided according to the quota allocations as stated above. The Brooklyn Museum should aim for the entire collection to reach these standards.

3) The Museum shall have an equal staff recruitment policy in relation to race/ethnicity which means that the positions advertised after the agreement has been signed should be divided according to the following quota allocations: 20% Caucasian/white, 25% Asian/Pacific Islander, 25% Latin American/Hispanic, 25% African-American/black, 5% other. The Brooklyn Museum should have as a long term goal to mirror, across salary levels,

3. Self-Definition decides which Subject Position Category (SPC) in regard to gender the artist, author performer, lecturer, staff member etc. belongs to.
4. The Brooklyn Museum should to the greatest degree strive to fill the quota allocations as stated originally and aim at avoiding making Alternative Quota Allocations (AQA). If this, in few and specific situations is impossible, AQA is to be carried out under strict supervision and monitoring by TSC.
5. Definition of ethnics group can be called from the U.S. Census Bureau https://www.census.gov/. Self-Definition decides which Subject Position Category (SPC) in regard to race/ethnicity the artist, performer, lecturer, staff member etc. belongs to.

the quota allocations as stated above. The Brooklyn Museum should strive to avoid stereotypical race/ethnicity roles in its staff recruitment policy.

4) Alternative Quota Allocations (AQA) in relation to race/ethnicity[6] - If the quota 20% Caucasian/white cannot be filled, space can be allocated to persons choosing to define themselves as Asian/Pacific Islander, Latin American/Hispanic, African-American/black or other. If the quota 25% Asian/Pacific Islander cannot be filled, space can only be allocated to persons choosing to define themselves as Latin American/Hispanic, African-American/black or other. If the quota 25% Latin American/Hispanic cannot be filled, space can only be allocated by persons choosing to define themselves as Asian/Pacific Islander, African-American/black or other. If the quota 25% African-American/black cannot be filled, space can only be allocated to persons choosing to define themselves as Asian/Pacific Islander, Latin American/Hispanic or other. If the quota 5% other cannot be filled, space can only be allocated to persons choosing to define themselves as Asian/Pacific Islander, Latin American/Hispanic or African-American/black.

C. EQUAL PRACTICE IN RELATION CLASS PRIVILEGE[7]
1) The Museum shall have an equal exhibition programming in relation to class privilege which means that the authors of the works exhibited should be divided according to the following quota allocations: 35 % middle class, 0 % filthy rich, 10 % upper class, 20 % underclass, 35 % working class.

2) The Museum shall have an equal acquisition policy in relation to class privilege which means that the authors of the acquired works should be divided according to the following quota allocations: 35 % middle class, 0 % filthy rich, 10 % upper class, 20 % under class, 35% working class. The acquisition budget should be divided according to the quota allocationsas stated above. The Brooklyn Museum should aim for the entire collection to reach these standards.

3) The Museum shall have an equal staff recruitment policy in relation to class privilege which means that the positions advertised after the Agreement has been signed should be divided according to the following quota allocation: 35% middle class, 0% filthy rich, 10% upper class, 20% under class, 35% working class. The Brooklyn Museum should have as a long term goal to mirror, across salary levels, the quota allocations as stated above.

4) The Alternative Quota Allocations (AQA) in relation to class privilege[8] - If the quota 35% middle class cannot be filled, space can only be allocated to persons choosing to define themselves as under class or working class. If the quota 10 % upper class cannot be filled, space can only be allocated to persons choosing to define themselves as under class or working class. If the quota 20% under class cannot be filled, space can only be allocated by persons choosing to define themselves as

6. The Brooklyn Museum should to the greatest degree strive to fill the quota allocations as stated originally and aim at avoiding making Alternative Quota Allocations (AQA). If this, in few and specific situations is impossible, AQA is to be carried out under strict supervision and monitoring by TSC.

7. Self-Definition decides which Subject Position Category (SPC) in regard to class privilege the artist, author, performer, lecturer, staff member etc. belongs to. Brooklyn Museum should strive to avoid stereotypical class roles in its staff recruitment policy.

8. The Brooklyn Museum should to the greatest degree strive to fill the quota allocations as stated originally and aim at avoiding making Alternative Quota Allocations (AQA). If this, in few and specific situations is impossible, AQA is to be carried out under strict supervision and monitoring by TSC.

working class. If the quota 35 % working class cannot be filled, space can only be allocated to persons choosing to define themselves as under class.

D. EQUAL PRACTICE IN RELATION TO SEXUAL ORIENTATION[9]

1) The Museum shall have an equal exhibition programming in relation to sexual orientation which means that the authors of the works exhibited should be divided according to the following quota allocations: 30% heterosexual, 30% homosexual, 30% bisexual, 10% asexual.

2) The Museum shall have an equal acquisition policy in relation to sexual orientation which means that the authors of the acquired works should be divided according to the following quota allocations: 30% heterosexual, 30% homosexual, 30% bisexual, 10% asexual.

3) The Museum shall have an equal staff recruitment policy in relation to sexual orientation which means that the positions advertised after the agreement has been signed should be divided according to the following quota allocations: 30% heterosexual, 30% homosexual, 30% bisexual, 10% asexual. The Brooklyn Museum should have as a long term goal to mirror, across salary levels, the quota allocations as stated above. The Brooklyn Museum should strive to avoid stereotypical sexual orientation roles in its staff recruitment policy.4) Alternative Quota Allocations (AQA) in relation to sexual orientation[10] - If the quota 30% heterosexual cannot be filled, space can be allocated to persons choosing to define themselves as homosexual, bisexual or asexual. If the quota 30% homosexual cannot be filled, space can only be allocated to persons choosing to define themselves as bisexual or asexual. If the quota 30% bisexual cannot be filled, space can only be allocated by persons choosing to define themselves as homosexual or asexual. If the quota 10% asexual cannot be

E. THEMATIC RESTRICTIONS for persons with specific intersection of specific SPCs.

1) If a person, through Self-Definition chooses to identify with all of the following Subject Position Categories (SPC): man, Caucasian/white, heterosexual, middle- or upper class, that person will have thematic restrictions, and is only allowed to: In the case of being an artist, author or performer; present art work, or other work that deals with problematizing this group's privilege or in some other way draw attention to the damage inflicted by racist, sexist, capitalist, heteronormative structures. In the case of being a lecturer or seminar participant; present lectures or views that deal with problematizing this group's privilege or in some other way draw attention to the damage inflicted by racist, sexist, capitalist, heteronormative structures. In the case of being a staff member; work towards problematizing this group's privilege or in some other way draw attention to the damage inflicted by racist, sexist, capitalist, heteronormative structures, in all parts of the museum structures and operations that the person has access to.

9 . Self-Definition decides which Subject Position Category (SPC) in regard to sexual orientation the artist, performer, lecturer, staff member etc. belongs to.

10. The Brooklyn Museum should to the greatest degree strive to fill the quota allocations as stated originally and aim at avoiding making Alternative Quota Allocations (AQA). If this, in few and specific situations is impossible, AQA is to be carried out under strict supervision and monitoring by TSC. filled, space can only be allocated to persons choosing to define themselves as homosexual or bisexual.

F. EVALUATION

1) Brooklyn Museum's actions, which include exhibitions and other programming, acquisitions, staff recruitment policies, public outreach policies regarding museum visitors and participants in its educational programs will be evaluated every two years. The first Evaluation will take place two years following the date of the execution of this Agreement. The next Evaluation will take place after another two years, and so on. The agreement has no expiry date. The Evaluation is carried out in two steps and ends with a Public Hearing (PH) and a Verdict followed by the execution of a New Plan of Action (NPA). The Evaluation process will end with a party in the Grand Hall in the heart of the Brooklyn Museum organized and financed by the Brooklyn Museum.

2) The Special Committee (TSC) - The first step of the Evaluation is conducted by The Special Committee (TSC). TSC consists of Judith Butler, Gayatri Chakravorty Spivak and Cornel West, who have agreed to work on a contract basis for the Brooklyn Museum. TSC will closely follow and supervise the work of the Brooklyn Museum and be in dialogue on a monthly basis. Their main responsibility is to influence the Brooklyn Museum to be in compliance with this agreement. Furthermore, they are responsible for supporting, discussing and in very few cases scrutinizing each person's (persons belonging to the groups mentioned under WHEREAS I, ii) process of Self-Definition regarding which SPC the person chooses to identify with, and to monitor and report to the Brooklyn Museum in case a person decides to change SPC during the length of time the person is involved with the Brooklyn Museum, for example as an exhibiting artist, lecturer or staff member and consequently control the AQA procedure in case the quota allocations for certain SPCs are being over-run due to a person's change of SPC as stated above. Compare footnotes no 4, 6, 8 and 10. TSC will participate in the Public Hearing (PH) that takes place during the Evaluation and present their work through a PowerPoint presentation.

3) The Artist Committee (TAC) - The second step of the Evaluation is conducted by The Artist Committee (TAC). TAC consists of 50 local and international artists chosen by the YES!. Their task is to be in dialogue with TSC and the Brooklyn Museum before and during the Evaluation and to give direct feedback and suggestions on the two years work and results of the Brooklyn Museum's efforts to comply with this agreement. TAC will participate in the Public Hearing (PH) that takes place during the Evaluation and present their research through a lecture. Each TAC member will receive a fee by the Brooklyn Museum (sum to be negotiated separately under the supervision of the YES!).

4) Public Hearing (PH) - The third step in the Evaluation is a Public Hearing (PH) held at the Grand Hall in the heart of the Brooklyn Museum. All Inhabitants of the Borough of Brooklyn (AIBB) are invited to hear the TSC and the TAC give their view on the work of the Brooklyn Museum in relation to this agreement. The floor is then open to discussion, questions, suggestions, objections and comments from the AIBB.

5) Verdict - At the end of the PH the three parties: TSC, TAC and AIBB will vote on whether Brooklyn Museum is in compliance with this agreement or not. Their Verdict is final and cannot be appealed.

6) New Plan of Action (NPA) - After the PH and the Verdict (regardless of the out-come of the Verdict) TSC and TAC will work together and be responsible for presenting a New Plan of Action (NPA). The NPA should stake out the direction that the Brooklyn Museum

should take for the next two years and suggest concrete demands in order to comply with this Agreement. When formulating the NPA, all thoughts, suggestions and objections expressed by the AIBB during the PH should be taken under consideration.

7) The Evaluation process, the presentations, the PH, the Verdict and the final presentation of the NPA, will proceed until the three parties; TSC, TAC and AIBB have agreed. The Brooklyn Museum will provide high quality food and drinks and a per diem allowance of 500 USD to everybody participating in the PH and thereby consulting the Brooklyn Museum on how to become a better museum.

8) If, at the Verdict, the Brooklyn Museum is found not to be in compliance with this Agreement, the TSC and/or the TAC and/or the AIBB will not be held accountable and no legal or financial consequences will follow on their part. However, members of the TSC could be exchanged if the TAC considers that they have not lived up to their responsibilities and members of the TAC could be exchanged if the AIBB considers that they have not lived up to their responsibilities. The Brooklyn Museum is responsible for administering and implementing these changes following the YES!'s recommendations on substitute members.

ARTICLE 6 - LIQUIDATED DAMAGES

6.1 If, after Evaluation, the Brooklyn Museum is found through the verdict by TSC, TAC and AIBB not to be in default of its obligations under this Agreement, the Brooklyn Museum shall pay liquidated damages in the amount of Ten Thousand U.S. Dollars (USD 10,000), to be adjusted yearly by percentage in relation to inflation, for each percentage of deficient distribution in regards to gender, race/ethnicity, class privilege or sexual orientation within the exhibition- and other programming, acquisitions and staff recruitment. The amount is payable to YES!'s fund, which has been established to make the world more diverse, equal and interesting.

6.2 In the event that the Museum is found to be in default, YES! agrees to be in dialogue with the TSC, TAC and AIBB regarding how this money should be most effectively distributed or spent. YES! also agrees to take responsibility for paying themselves a moderate fee from this fund for their work with making the world more diverse, equal and interesting, and having to counteract the failure of the Brooklyn Museum on their mission to do the same.

ARTICLE 7 - EXCEPTION

If the terms of this agreement have not been fulfilled and the failure is due to the Museums's duties as prescribed by employment legislation, the Brooklyn Museum will not be held accountable.

ARTICLE 8 - APPLICABLE LAWS

This Agreement shall be governed by and construed in accordance with the laws of the State of New York, without regard to its conflicts of laws provisions. The Parties, in performance of this Agreement, shall comply with all applicable local, state, and federal laws, orders, rules, regulations, and ordinances.

ARTICLE 9 - ASSIGNMENT
Any assignment of the Parties' rights or duties shall be void, unless prior written consent
is given by the other Party.

IN WITNESS WHEREOF, YES! and the Brooklyn Museum have executed this
agreement as of the date and year first hereinabove written and have each a copy of
this agreement. The Brooklyn Museum and YES! are bound to this agreement upon
ratification by the Brooklyn Museum's representatives and YES!'s representatives.

SIGNATURES:

For THE BROOKLYN MUSEUM:

For YES! ASSOCIATION/FÖRENINGEN JA!:

Johanna Gustavsson, Artist
Hong-An Truong, Artist
Åsa Elzén, Artist
Malin Arnell, Artist

LETTER TO MARINETTI:
TO LIBERATE ONESELF FROM ECSTACY OF
CONSUMING AND TO DISCOVER THE FUTURE (2009)

ARAHMAIANI

Dear Marinetti,

To speak about the future with the passion and optimism that you had in your life has currently become nearly impossible to accept and to do. After 100 years of passing time, what you dreamed of as a world of "beautiful speed" has turned into "speed that misleads and brings suffering". Maybe you could not imagine this dark side because then imagination and fantasy had not yet grasped it. Speed has now proceeded without control or direction. It has penetrated space and time which was formerly considered to be sacred and pure by those who wish the mystery of life to continue to birth dreams and hope. It has made the world rush helter-skelter without direction. It is as if life has slipped into a space characterized by darkness. The people of Java used this character as a time signifier, and describe it as the times of madness.

True, the idea of progress has birthed acceleration and machines have also created a world full of "wonders". It is as if distances and time have been shortened. It is as if everything is moving fast and efficiently, which at a glance appears to be progressive and so wonderful. The world appears to have shrunk, it has become small — there are no more mysterious places that cannot be reached and discovered. It is as if everything in life and in the universe can now be conquered and controlled. The human being has become the being who sits on the pinnacle of the hierarchy and is permitted to decide where life might be taken and directed to. The shroud of mystery seems to have been completely opened and every answer to every question seems to have been found. But in reality, is it really that way? Does life only offer a limited dimension, merely revealing a handsome face and not revealing another, terrifying face?

The thundering sound of machines which used to signify hope in the future and paradise have now become the thundering sound of anger and destruction. Exploding with shattering sound as murderous machines in the killing fields of the poor and powerless. Or it has become the thundering sound of factory machines that exploit human beings and reduces them to become mere extensions of production means. The machine which you saw as the vehicle that would carry humankind towards enlightenment and a golden age in reality has brought about disasters and tempests. Machines which should help humankind to raise its dignity have now devoured their creators. And wars that depend on various murder machines have now become blatant brutality aimed at multiplying profit.

It seems that those times of promises and dreams have now passed. Science and sophisticated technology has been employed unwisely, they have merely become instruments of power; supports for the fundamental market system. They have failed to answer the challenges of life on planet earth which is being flailed by violence and poverty. Machines have also thrown up all sorts of poisons and hazardous wastes that have choked life's breathing apparatus, destroyed the natural environment, punctured the ozone layer and strangled humanity, creating wondering zombies. They have become beings without conscience and without feelings, who are always ready to consume anything in their reach. And to do this they will not shrink from murdering and torturing other human beings.

These zombies wear many types of caps and attributes. They can be greedy businessmen or conglomerates who skillfully manipulate consumers who can also bring themselves to burn entire countries to the ground or destroy anything for profit. They can be politicians who hunger for power and who will justify any means to achieve their ambitions. They also have no shame to lick the butts of the conglomerates to receive funds for campaigns and propaganda of the political ideology of whatever-as-long-as-they-have-power. Or they can also appear as intellectuals and religious leaders who pawn and sell their knowledge and their faith in order to be able to lovingly caress power and money.

Power and material things have become potent and intoxicating thirst quenching wines! And under the pressure of the accumulation of material dreams, humanity has gagged its own freedom and its own source of life. The earth is raped, water is wasted and polluted, forests are chopped down and burnt, the soil is poisoned. And everything inside it is consumed and exploited till the end. As if there will be no future coming. The important thing is that today we can swallow and fill our bellies as full as we can and reap as much profit as possible. Time is money and time must be used to seize opportunities to fulfill our needs as soon as right now, because delay means missing opportunities and that means not behaving in accordance to the demands of the times.

The world has now become a village — people can travel from one continent to another in a relatively short time. Places and time have been condensed. Human beings from various social and cultural backgrounds can meet as if differences are no longer an issue. Geographic boundaries have dissolved but mental and psychological gaps have widened and deepened, forming vulgar hierarchical rankings. Life is now divided as such; on one side there is a small group that "possesses special privileges" to obtain anything, in quantities of more than they need. And on the other side there is a large group who "have no rights whatsoever", who are only permitted to dig around in the garbage dumps of the specially privileged group. They also are obliged to offer their time and work to their bones for the welfare of the powerful people above them.

The structure of life has become a two tiered pyramid, where the upper level is lived in by the first group or the rulers who make sure that their standard of life style and civilization must be guaranteed to be special even though they must conduct violence and indulge in criminal ways to maintain that special standard. Meanwhile those who live in the lower level are those who live on the crumbs and leftovers from those upstairs. They also must live in crowded and cramped conditions because their number is great and the space available for them is insufficient. Of course they are also vulnerable to all sorts of bad luck, disease and ill fortune. The term human rights in reality is merely a slogan.

Art and culture

So where is art and culture placed? Part is in the dark lower level of the pyramid and part is used as decoration in the lives of those upstairs, placed in special or private halls that cannot be entered by just anybody! Art becomes objects, things to multiply wealth — art becomes a means of investment that decorate the sterile walls of auction houses and commercial galleries. Or art is imprisoned in museums to keep company with the ghosts of the past who are drowning in sorrow and shackled by loneliness. Art is alienated from its society and also from its creator — art becomes a mere representation and a spectacle that is to be consumed, it is an image that is porced from life, isolated from reality.

The world that is controlled by the power of capital and often transforms into tyranny has birthed the consumerist and passive life style on a global scale. Humankind has been alienated from itself and also from other human beings. The same has happened in the art world — the artist is swept by the tide of self surrender to the symbolic power that determines the conditions and the classifications of what is termed "art". Art is considered to be "too important" and the artist is ensnared in the trap! So the artist loses her freedom and has reins put on her! Now, art seems to be a burden and a shackle that binds the wings of creativity to prevent them from flying freely!

Obviously this is an extremely absurd situation: art no longer has any connection to life and merely supports the financial market, it is glorified and placed high on a pedestal, it is imprisoned in a place deemed to be secure! Meanwhile, life is slowly being destroyed and humankind is being exterminated through wars and environmental destruction. Indeed, the hard, macho, boots of military soldiers have stomped on our heads and chopped down our conscience to make it bland. Their troops of armored tanks have surged forward to destroy the palace of common sense and are now moving menacingly to completely obliterate the monument of humanity that stands straight before our restless and anxious thoughts.

The bombs that explode in the corners of cities or in the sacred places of Muslims have obliterated the forms of civilizations that were constructed through millennia in a blink of the eye. The sound wakes us up from our slumber and our long dream of eternal life — it has disturbed the Sphinx that has been silent for centuries. It has ripped apart all fantasy and dreams of wisdom, belief, faith, and compassion. It has turned values upside down and created terror upon terror in a never ending life of suffering. It haunts long and exhausting days that are filled with fear and uncertainty. It is as if the pyramid of faith and honesty has also been upturned and now it is spilling tears while it sings a never ending Elegy that has made the Eye swell forever.

The world has shrunk and is on the brink of shattering because of speed! Honestly — now is the time to reduce the speed which you used to think of as the symbol of liberation! Humanity must renew its vision and discover a new human sensitivity and a new human consciousness, to be able to respect the right to live and difference and to erase hierarchy. For the future, for to save the earth that is melting in the heat! Humanity must unite in the form of the highest consciousness based on intuition, which will provide free spaces for anyone to express herself in her own format and cultural experience. Then she will discover art that liberates from the talons of the shackles of the times!

Art must be able to free itself from the greedy claws of capital owners, from the manipulation of politicians who only employ power for their private interests or the interests of their group. Art must be free from all dogma and ideology. Art must stand independently and form an autonomous discourse and narrative — it must bring together different elements and possibilities so that a new awareness and a new sensitivity may break through the boundary walls and cut away the rope that binds imagination. An esthetics that stands on the culture of togetherness and the awareness of humanity and a new social perspective must be discovered! So a future that prioritizes a holistic life view that is sensitive to the environment may be built! Fantasy and imagination must not be tripped over and rendered impotent only by economic calculations. The dignity of humankind and life is more than mere economic calculations and mathematical equations.

When the blind faith in the unreliable dogma of the market can be shattered — it will be possible to imagine a future full of hope. Not like our current situation, where in reality humankind finds it difficult to visualize a future. Optimism is imprisoned in a coffin! A creative person might know where the key to the coffin is hidden. She might free the optimism which will then transform into the courage to say NO to every form of destruction of nature, greed, the disrespect to common sense and also to tyranny. She will clear the path and blaze the trail of change. She will release the shackles and the binds of fantasy and imagination and let them fly free and become the future of all the inhabitants of this planet earth. She will become hope for those who still wish to continue life.

The "futurism" of this day will be based on a complete renewal of the awareness of humanity and justice. It will be a celebration of the arrivals of new, needed practical technologies and discoveries of new outlooks and new formulations and definitions in the field of science. The dynamics of "connections" between the elements of life will become a very important science (so that sciences will no longer be isolated in specialized boxes). And the artist will be the first person who must implement this knowledge in her esthetical concepts and her artistic practice. So art will be able to be present in the midst of life and find a correct reason to justify being there. Art will be a source of "enlightenment" — the artist will be a person who bears the torch in the frontline of the long and winding path of life.

Art must become the possession of all people. All elements who to date have been marginalized, the poor, the colored skinned, minorities and women, must be given a space and opportunities to produce and enjoy works of art. So it is not only those who have the means to purchase and those who have power over the bureaucracy who are free to enjoy and explore the products of creativity and monopolize production and distribution. Women, particularly, need not hide behind simplicity or the image of luxury to be able to express themselves. The real woman, the woman who represents the future, is the woman who stands on her own two feet and is capable of expressing and giving meaning to her own sexuality, eroticism, and her own reproductive system. She is also free to determine the form and meaning of her individual esthetics, such as determining her relationship with her partner in accordance to her desire and hopes based on the principle of mutual agreement.

In short, basically, the world and the esthetical values which to date have been controlled by very masculine powers and energies too much, must be balanced by the feminine. The phallus-centric era and the power of the patriarchy must be ended. The principle of androgyny will color life and art in the future. The fall of the World Trade Center in New York City, bombed and destructed by who-knows-who, is a sign that the financial system must be changed and the structure of the dominant thinking must be deconstructed. The system based on fossil fuels — those materials that have become the source of conflict — must be rethought and reanalyzed — alternative energy sources must take their place. If not the earth will burn to cinders and dry up, half its inhabitants will die of hunger. Art, no longer having any meaning, will be reduced to nauseating decoration.

Human beings will die but art should — as an age old adage says — be eternal. And to become eternal art must touch on things that are basic to life. Art must have the courage to leave everything that is established in its time, burst through the boundaries and enter the "unknown regions". The cultural jungle of spectacles created by the system to render all the residents of earth impotent, to conquer them in order so that all obey and follow the rules of the "consumer society" must be passed through! So that the eyes that are swollen from lengthy weeping because of the disaster that has struck relentlessly will be able to see through and open the layers of shrouds of the mirage of reality. Art should function as a "means" with which to examine and assess reality. Art must be capable of fanning the spirit of liberation like a bonfire that never burns out!

For the people of Java when the earth is shaken by quakes and volcanoes cough and discharge flaming clouds, that is nature's reaction to something that is wrong in life. The earth is saddened and angry that humanity is only interested in extracting and consuming her wealth. Never wanting to nurture her let alone returning her kindness. Intellect is drowned in hot and toxic mud that has erupted over on to the surface of the earth because humankind does not care about the consequences of their actions. Creativity is only aimed at things that give immediate and temporary satisfaction. Artworks are manufactured and managed according to the mechanisms of a factory. Garbage esthetics are mass produced and pile up in gardens of artificial beauty. And serenaded by systematic hymns of seduction that penetrate the soul, humankind is forced to swallow that garbage. Humankind is being stoned by loneliness in the midst of the clamor of retinal sensations and consumer ecstasy, towards moksa and eternal nirvana.

(The future cannot be created without weighing what is happening now, even more by killing and denying the past).

July 2009.

MANIFESTO OF THE SCEPTICS (2009)

ARAHMAIANI

Apparently, the term "contemporary art" triggers never ending discussions and debates — whether it is in a particular Indonesian context, or an Asian, or a worldwide context in general. A consequence of this is the effort to map the situation, with an assumption based on a theory of hegemony: The West dominates the rest! Maybe there is some truth in this, though if we look at the latest developments we should begin to think that slowly this theory is starting to crumble, to be taken to pieces.

Artists continuously discuss issues of identity, they question their "cultural position" in the global cultural formation and dialogue. Art practices reflect the effort to discover "identity" — this is obvious. But on the other hand the process of giving meaning to "identity" has also become extremely complicated — especially when it is challenged by the latest market system which can "devour" nearly every cultural product and turn it into a mere commodity!

The rapid development of information and communication technologies means that artists who live in the backwaters of a certain continent have the opportunity to create relationships with other artists in other parts of other continents. So the situation in which artists influence each other in styles of expression, ideas and concepts, is developing very fast. Connections in the virtual world and digital technology have made what was thought to be impossible, a reality.

These "new mediums" are being continuously developed — the potentials that have a "liberating" nature must be explored even further. Our current world which is controlled through the manipulations of images and spectacles can be "neutralized" with digital technology and the virtual world which are not so easy to place an ownership claim over. Technology has made anyone able to duplicate and multiply. This means that a centralized control is close to impossible to enforce, but control of power can be done and monopolies might become history!

So we continue our discussions, we try to give even further meaning to the idea of "an expanded definition of art" — expand it as wide as possible! We must explore work strategies so that art does not become a noose without us realizing it, without us feeling it, just because we are enthralled with the games and the pleasure of the visual sensations of the images that we create. Consciously or not we surrender to the flow of pleasure and we avoid issues and conflicts. Probably our excuse is that we don't want to create more problems or we don't want to hurt people's feelings.

True, we must avoid and even condemn any council to make war — to kill and destroy each other. But this doesn't mean that we must avoid conflict and difference in opinion. A democratic system should be able to accommodate and manage conflicts and differences in opinions. Conflicts and dissent do not have to be handled through a "security" approach and with the use of violence — dialog and negotiations in equality is the procedure to find solutions and solve problems.

While we were enwrapped in discussion suddenly it was as if wild waves began to toss us around while we were sailing, the earth shook without control. The thunderous sound from the bowels of the earth intensified the gripping atmosphere which was followed by completely uncontrollable panic! At that time the morning had just broken to greet the world, and the quiet of the youthful morning was ripped in an instance. Those who were already awake or had not yet gone to sleep scattered to avoid the buildings that were crumbling down. In less than 1 minute our district was devastated by an earthquake and 4000 lives were sent home to eternity!

(I was involved in a virtual discussion, thousands of kilometers away — suddenly I lost contact and connection)

Manifesto of the Sceptics

1.	Our art is an autonomous zone — a self standing discourse and narrative. It cannot be dictated to by the interests of the market, politics or religion. Businessmen, politicians and religious leaders are not creators of art!

2.	Our art belongs to everyone — everyone has the right to express themselves. This means that artists should not surrender to the symbolic powers that determine the conditions and the classification of art.

3.   Our art must not be separated from life and become mere decoration. Art must be able to encourage a new awareness of humanity and a new social consciousness.

4.   Our art is not an object — art is a neutral medium with the function of offering alternative values, changing values, and also turning values upside down. So art is capable of forming new values and bringing down those which are established!

5.   Our art is a type of "alchemical vessel" — a vessel that can combine the sacred and the profane in one discourse that is capable of uniting contradicting elements. It can create a meeting point between the material and the spiritual, between the masculine and the feminine.

6.   Our art is a channel for creativity — like plumbing that supplies fresh water. And creativity, like water, is an active force that is the essence of life which births ideas and concepts. In other words, a liberating force!

7.   Our art is a natural, sustainable process — sowing seed, germinating, and producing fruit.

8.   Our art is a "tool" to examine and assess reality, and can be employed by anyone, anytime, and anywhere!

9.   Our art connects the past, the present, and the future.

10.   Our art is a combination of courage, rebellion, rational and moral intelligence, and the conscience.

11.   Although we are orientated forward, our art remembers and considers the past and the present.

12.   The definition of art must be expanded — as wide as it possibly can be!

Yogyakarta, July 2009.

Arahmaiani.

Der Sex ist im Text

I'll say it straight away – SEX is something special. You won't agree with me. Nevertheless language is also in a perpetual state of flux and the number of women who play a part in determining the language that we speak is increasing. The number is growing just as women's bodies in general have been designed for expansion and reproduction. To put your sperm inside here, that is man's desire. Still in 2009, impressed with towers, the money machine is falling apart unfortunately but reproduction remains. We need to talk again. We have to talk about how we solve this problem with the MONEY. No more quick promises, we want the realities. Invest more in real estate, but then the endless new properties stand empty, therefore we need paintings to fill these properties with meaning. Or refugees. Migrants are always grateful for the large number of empty real estate speculation projects. How much space does a person need and can he pay for it? Can he pay for the image of a person. So you pay me for my picture. No, this sort of thing doesn't actually belong in a press release, I just wanted to seduce you to buy one of my works. With my charm, my evening gown and my biography, I wanted to seduce you into buying a painting from me. You can google me and you can see just how much I've accomplished in the last 20 years, what I'm still accomplishing and how much I'll accomplish next year. I'm a good investment because I work for you. In my evening gown. The price of the evening gown is included in the painting, one evening gown per painting, No, you mustn't pay for my dinner, that is always the question, who's paying whom, who is the better conversationalist, are you getting on my nerves or are you seducing me into your beautiful collector's world – how well you can describe the works in your collection – now you have to come out at the table, provide information, to a woman, yes, to a woman, but you could buy one of the silent paintings, they only demand something from you once, then they leave you more or less in peace for the rest of your life, and I and my gallery owners work for their value, that's ultimately actually a part of your value. That's how you and I both become more valuable. Why don't I tell you anything about the women? Since when have you had an interest in women – I mean genuinely? An interest in their biographies and needs? You have one to show? Fair enough perhaps my woman appeals to your wife? Perhaps your wife sees herself in my woman? These days women participate in the decision making with a purchase or are you a self employed woman? Then you certainly understand how difficult it is to earn money under certain circumstances. No, you say, for you it is quite easy, I am a collector and I come from Hannover. A filly. In most cases a horse costs more than a painting, unless you just want to eat the horse. No, the painting you can't eat, even if you're very hungry. SEX helps to get through of few days of fasting, but then it gets serious.

Elke Krystufek
April 2009

THE GUERRILLA GIRLS' GUIDE TO BEHAVING BADLY
(which you have to do most of the time in the world as we know it) (2010)

SCHOOL OF THE ART INSTITUTE OF CHICAGO
COMMENCEMENT ADDRESS
MAY 22 2010

I bet this is the first time a woman wearing a gorilla mask has ever given a commencement address. If this makes it into *Ripley's Believe it or Not*, the School of the Art Institute of Chicago should get an award for taking the leap. It's delicious that an anonymous, masked artist is speaking to you today, when the art world still clings to the outmoded idea that art has to be about the individual — one great genius after another, creating entirely original work, passing the mantle on to the next genius, forming a master narrative that tells the history of our culture. And, ok, these geniuses are mostly pale and mostly male. So, what are the rest of us, including the 67% of Art Institute students who happen to be female, to do?

In 1985, we got the idea to put up two posters on the streets of NY about the state of women artists in the New York Art world. It wasn't a pretty picture. But we had a philosophy about how to construct political art — to twist an issue around and present it in a way that hadn't been seen before.

Who knew that our work would cause all hell to break loose? Who knew it would cause a major crisis of conscience about diversity in the art world, a subject museums, collectors and critics had ignored and denied for a long, long time. Now, it's a no brainer.... you can't tell the story of a culture without all the voices in it. Who knew that those two posters would lead to hundreds of others, plus actions, billboards, sticker and books — not just about about art, but about women and people of color in the worlds of film, politics and pop culture. Who knew that 25 years later we — the agitating outsiders — would wind up inside the museums we criticize: the Art Institute, The Museum of Modern Art in NY, the Pompidou in Paris... and be speaking to all of you today. The Guerrilla Girls have been so lucky to do this work and we're so grateful that thousands of people all over the world, aged 8 to 80, write to us each year telling us that we inspired them to become activists, too.

We were just a bunch of girls who couldn't put up and shut up. We saw something that needed to be done. And we figured out a way to do it. We didn't have a plan but we had attitude and a strategy. We know that each of you in the Class of 2010 want to do great creative work and have strategies and attitude, too. We know you want to be the best artists, designers, writers, administrators, architects, and educators you can be. But we also know that you want to do good in the world at the same time. We all have to.

We can't not.

36

So today, as you go out to transform the worlds of art, design, fashion, architecture, art history, writing, critical theory, etc, plus fields that haven't been invented yet, I want to share some things we learned along the way.

Presenting: THE GUERRILLA GIRLS' GUIDE TO BEHAVING BADLY (which you have to do most of the time in the world as we know it) (2010)

GUERRILLA GIRLS

Be a loser. The world of art and design doesn't have to be an Olympics where a few win and everyone else is forgotten. Even though the art market and celebrity culture is set up to support the idea of hyper-competition and to make everyone but the stars feel like failures, there's also a world out there of artistic co-operation and collaboration that's not about raging egos. That's the one we joined, and the one you can join, too. Get beyond the outdated assumption that only a handful of you will "make it." Don't all waste your time running after the same few carrots.

Be impatient. Don't wait for a stamp of approval from the system. Don't wait around to be asked to dance. Claim your place. Put on your own shows, create your own companies, develop your own projects. To steal a phrase from the Dali Lama, "Be the change you want to see in the world." In other words, Be the artworld you want to take part in.

Be crazy. Political art that just points to something and says "this is bad" is like preaching to the choir. Try to change people's minds about issues. Do it in an outrageous, unforgettable way. A lot of people in the art and film world didn't believe things were as bad as we said they were and we brought them around....with facts, humor and a little fake fur. Here's a trick we learned: If you can get someone who disagrees with you to you to laugh at an issue, you have a hook into their brain. Once inside you have a better chance of changing their minds.

Be anonymous. You'd be surprised what comes out of your mouth when you're wearing a gorilla mask. We started wearing them to protect our careers, but soon realized it was one of the secrets of our success. Anonymous free speech is protected by the First Amendment. So join that long line of anonymous masked avengers, like Robin Hood, Batman, and of course, Wonder Woman.

Be an outsider. Maybe having a secret identity isn't for you. But even if you end up working inside the system, act like an outsider. Look for the understory, the subtext, the overlooked, and the downright unfair, then expose it. We've empowered lots of people inside museums, universities and film studios to jam their culture and diss their institutions.

Lead a double life. Be a split personality. Be two, three, four, five artists in one body, like me. I'm an artist / activist / writer / graphic designer. Be a hybrid. Hybrids are so green.

Just do one thing. If it works, do another. If it doesn't, try it another way. Over time, we promise you it will all add up to something effective and great. Don't be paralyzed because you can't do it all right away. Just keep on chipping away.

Don't make only FINE art. Make some cheap art that can be owned by everyone, like books and movies can.

Sell out. If people start paying attention to you, don't waste time wondering if you've lost your edge. Take your critique right inside the galleries and institutions to a larger audience. When our work appears at venerable venues like the Venice Biennale, the Tate Modern, or The National Gallery in DC, we get hundreds of letters from people saying they were blown away by our analysis of art and culture.

Give collectors, curators, and museum directors tough love: (Bear with me, this is a long rant.) It's a pity that public art museums have to compete with billionaire art investors to own significant artworks. And then depend on those investors to donate the works! It's outrageous that art by women and artists of color sold at auction bring 10-20% of the price of art by white males. It's unethical that wealthy art collectors who put lots of money in the art market can then become museum trustees, overseeing museums that in turn validate their investments. What a lousy way to write and preserve our history! If things continue like they're going, a hundred years from now, many museums will be showing only the white male version of art history, with a few tokens thrown in. You need to keep that from happening. Make sure that museums cast a wider net and collect the real story of our culture.

How can you deliver tough love to the art world? Demand ethical standards inside museums. No more insider trading. No more conflicts of interest! No more cookie cutter collections of Art That Costs The Most (Eli Broad, do you hear us?) While you're at it, give some tough love to design and architecture, where women and people of color face a crushing glass ceiling. And finally, educators out there, don't teach a history constructed by corrupt institutions. Write your own!

Complain, complain, complain. But be creative about it. Sure we've done 45 feet high banners and billboards all over the world. But here's some simpler things we've done: Put anti-film industry stickers in movie theatre bathrooms, insert fliers with facts about art world discrimination into books in museum stores, send anonymous postcards to museum directors. Want more ideas? How about attaching political hangtags to items in clothing stores, putting up street art or billboards across from your office, slapping stickers on fashion magazine covers. You can probably think up a million better ideas than we can.

Use the F word. Be a feminist. For decades the majority of art school graduates have been women. Your class is no exception. But after school, when you find a too-small number of women and people of color in your field, especially at the top, then you know there's got to be discrimination, conscious or unconscious, going on. Don't just put up with it, say something. We think its ridiculous that so many people who believe in the tenets of feminism have been brainwashed by negative stereotypes in the media and society and refuse to call themselves feminists. And guys, that means you, too. Time to man up, whether you're female, male, trans, etc. and speak up for women. Women's rights, civil rights, and gay, lesbian and trans rights are the great human rights movements of our time. There's still a long way to go.

And last, but not least, be a great ape.

In 1917, Franz Kafka wrote a short story titled 'A Report to An Academy', in which an ape spoke about what it was like to be taken into captivity by a bunch of educated, intellectual types. The published story ends with the ape tamed and broken by the stultified academics. But in an earlier draft, Kafka tells a different story. The ape ends his report by instructing other apes NOT to allow themselves to be tamed. He says instead: "break the bars of your cages, bite a hole through them, squeeze through an opening…and ask yourself where do YOU want to go?"

Make that YOUR ending, not the tamed and broken one.

Oh...And don't forget to have some serious fun along the way!!!!

RELATIONAL FILMMAKING MANIFESTO (2010)

JULIE PERINI

Relational filmmakers do not make films about people.

Relational filmmakers make films with people.

Relational filmmakers do not interview subjects.

Relational filmmakers have conversations with other people.

Relational filmmakers do not know what the final film will look like.

Relational filmmakers make formal decisions that address the aesthetic, ethical, technical, and personal problems encountered throughout the making of the film.

Relational filmmakers do not adhere to established modes or conventions.

Relational filmmakers make films that are abstract, factual, and fictional, all at once.

Relational filmmakers do not fuck around with these tools of representation and power.

Relational filmmakers use their tools to experiment with new ways of being and to emancipate new forms of subjectivity.

Relational filmmakers believe that reality is the consequence of what we do together. Their films carry and conduct traces of this belief. Relational films are co-created through careful and playful interrogations of the roles performed by the people and materials involved with the film's production and reception: artists, subjects, passers-by, audiences, environments, ideas, and things.

ECOSEX MANIFESTO

(i) WE ARE THE ECOSEXUALS. The Earth is our lover. We are madly, passionately, and fiercely in love, and we are grateful for this relationship each and every day. In order to create a more mutual and sustainable relationship with the Earth, we collaborate with nature. We treat the Earth with kindness, respect and affection.

(ii) WE MAKE LOVE WITH THE EARTH. We are aquaphiles, terraphiles, pyrophiles and aerophiles. We shamelessly hug trees, massage the earth with our feet, and talk erotically to plants. We are skinny dippers, sun worshippers and stargazers. We caress rocks, are pleasured by waterfalls and admire the Earth's curves often. We make love to the Earth through our senses. We celebrate our E-spots. We are very dirty.

(iii) WE ARE A RAPIDLY GROWING GLOBAL COMMUNITY OF ECOSEXUALS. This community includes artists, academics, sex workers, sexologists, healers, environmental activists, nature fetishists, gardeners, business people, therapists, lawyers, peace activists, eco-feminists, scientists, educators, (r)evolutionaries, critters and other entities from all walks of life. Some of us are SexEcologists, researching and exploring the places where sexology and ecology intersect in our culture. As consumers we aim to buy less. When we must, we buy green, organic and local. Whether on farms, at sea, in the woods, or in small towns or large cities, we connect and empathize with nature.

(iv) WE ARE ECOSEX ACTIVISTS. We will save the mountains, waters and skies by any means necessary, especially through love, joy and our powers of seduction. We will stop the rape, abuse and the poisoning of the Earth. We do not condone the use of violence, although we recognize that some ecosexuals may choose to fight those most guilty for destroying the Earth with public disobedience, anarchist and radical environmental activist strategies. We embrace the revolutionary tactics of art, music, poetry, humor, and sex. We work and play tirelessly for Earth justice and global peace. Bombs hurt.

(v) ECOSEXUAL IS AN IDENTITY. For some of us being ecosexual is our primary (sexual) identity, whereas for others it is not. Ecosexuals can be GLBTQI, heterosexual, asexual, and/or Other. We invite and encourage ecosexuals to come out. We are everywhere. We are polymorphous and pollen-amorous. We educate people about ecosex culture, community and practices. We hold these truths to be self evident; that we are all part of, not separate from, nature. Thus all sex is ecosex.

(vi) THE ECOSEX PLEDGE. I promise to love, honor and cherish you Earth, until death brings us closer together forever.

VIVA LA ECOSEX REVOLUCION! JOIN US.

__________________   __________________

Elizabeth M. Stephens   Annie M. Sprinkle

80:20 (2011)
ANETTA MONA CHISA and LUCIA TKÁČOVÁ

80% OF REASONS TO BE HERE:

— SALAMI TACTICS WITHIN THE ART CONCERN
— TO FIGHT THE WAY THE WORLD MAP IS FOLDED
— CONFRONTATION, VERIFICATION, GRATIFICATION
— TO HIKE UP OUR PRICE
— TO SCORE
— TO BE SCENE & HERD
— ROMANCE IN THE AIR
— TO SPRITZ THE DAY OFF
— GOOD EXCUSE FOR MASSIVE OUTFIT SHOPPING
— + ON ARTFACTS
— TO HIT ALL THE COOL PARTIES
— PERFORMING HISTORY
— TO PUSSIFY THE BIENNALE
— TO HAVE THE CHANCE TO SAY ALL OF THIS OUT

20% OF REASONS NOT TO BE HERE:

— INVISIBILITY IS RESISTANCE
— NOT TO DECORATE THE GARDENS OF THE WHITE MALE
— BECAUSE JAN VERWOERT SAID "FORGET THE NATIONAL"
AND WE LIKE HIM
— VENICE BIENNALE = SHOWROOM OF WESTERN HEGEMONY
— GUILT
— NOT TO JEOPARDIZE OUR PLACE ON THE BARRICADES
— ART = REVOLUTION = SPECTACLE = CAPITAL
— BECAUSE WE ARE 1 COMMUNIST + 1 SOCIALIST FEMINIST
— ANTINOMADISM
— VENICE BIENNALE IS A CHOKING–ON–MONEY
MERCANTILIST FOSSIL
— THE ZOO EFFECT
— WE HAVE NOTHING TO WEAR FOR THE OPENING
— IT'S EASIER TO CRITICIZE A SHOW WHEN YOU'RE NOT IN IT
— THE CURSE OF BOOSTED EXPECTATIONS (2ND NOVEL
SYNDROME)
— TO KEEP OFF WHO'S HOT & WHO'S NOT
— TOURIST MENU SUCKS
— TO MAKE ART THE WAY WE FEEL, WITHOUT CONSIDERING
ITS POTENTIAL TO SUCCEED

MONEY IS GREEN TOO MANIFESTO (2011)

1. ALMOST ALL MONEY IS PAPER. THINK TWICE BEFORE CREATING A WAY
TO SPEND MORE & MORE MONEY BECAUSE THEN YOU COMPROMISE A TREE.

2. SOME MONEY IS IN THE FORM OF PLASTIC CARDS. THINK TWICE BEFORE
CREATING A PERSONAL NEED TO HAVE MORE TOXIC PLASTIC IN YOUR LIFE.

3. CREDIT CARDS ARE TO BE SEEN AS EQUIVALENCIES. THAT IS, IF WHAT IS
VISUALIZED INSIDE THE CARD AS A REAL ASSET IS TRULY THERE, THEN USE
THE CARD. IF WHAT IS VISUALIZED INSIDE THE CARD IS A PROBABILITY,
THEN DON'T USE THE CARD.

4. MONETARILY DO UNTO OTHERS AS WAS DONE BY OUR GRANDFATHERS.
THAT IS, OUR FATHERS AND GRANDFATHERS SPENT ONLY WHAT THEY HAD.
FOLLOW THEIR EXAMPLE. IF YOU DON'T HAVE IT, DON'T SPEND IT.

5. DO UNTO OTHERS AS YOU WANT DONE UNTO YOU. BEFORE YOU MAX
OUT A CARD, THINK OF THE TRIED AND TRUE AMERICAN WORKING THREE
JOBS TO PAY OFF YOUR MONETARY EXCESSES. SPEND THREE MINUTES A DAY
BEING SOMEBODY ELSE. THAT IS, BE THIS PERSON WITH 3 JOBS IN YOUR
IMAGINATION AND THEN DECIDE WHAT TO DO.

6. THE GOVERNMENT IS HYPNOTIZING US TO BE FINANCIALLY CARELESS,
EXCESSIVE AND IRRESPONSIBLE. IT IS A PLOY AND WAY FOR THEM TO THEN
DO A POLITICAL INTERVENTION AND PUNISHMENT THAT HAS
CONSEQUENCES THAT ARE TO BE FEARED.

7. "I WILL MAX OUT MY CARD BECAUSE I'M TERMINALLY ILL" IS A MONEY
SIN AKIN TO ANYTHING YOU MIGHT CONSIDER A SIN IN YOUR INDIVIDUAL
CONSCIENCE. WHY? BECAUSE SOMEBODY'S HARD WORKING BROTHER WILL
HAVE TO EVENTUALLY PAY FOR YOUR DEBTS.

8. BANKRUPTCY IS THE INQUISITION OF THE MIDDLE CLASS: THE "WORKER"
TAKES UP THE SLACK OF THE "WANTER".

9. DO ONLY WHAT YOU CAN AFFORD.

10. WANT ONLY WHAT YOU CAN AFFORD. IF YOU HAVE ENOUGH MONEY AND HAVE BECOME AN ADDICTED WANTER, THEN ASK, WHY WANT?

11. TRANSLATED, THAT SAYS: ASK, WHY DO I WANT WHAT I HAVE BEEN HYPNOTIZED TO WANT?

12. STOP IMAGINING YOU HAVE MONEY WHEN YOU DON'T. IF YOU DON'T HAVE MONEY, GET A JOB AND LIVE IN A WAY THAT SUPPORTS YOU, NOT A WAY THAT SUPPORTS A HABIT THAT IS AN ELITIST AFFRONT TO YOUR SOUL.

13. MONEY IS ONE OF LIFE'S TABOOS LIKE SEX, DEATH. MONEY IS IN THE PROCESS OF BEING DE-TABOOED, BUT IS NOW AT THE LAUGHINGSTOCK/ FOOL STAGE OF DE-CONSTRUCTION. BY TAKING MONEY SERIOUSLY, IT WILL BE REINSTATED TO ITS PREVIOUS POSITION OF RESPECT / KIND-CARE AND WILL HAVE SURVIVED THE TEST OF TABOO.

14. ASK: ARE LOVE AND MONEY OXYMORONONIC OR CONGRUENT? WHAT ABOUT COMMODIFIED / SATISFIED? SUSTAINABLE / WASTEFUL? BARTER / BUY? GENEROUS / HOARDING?

15. THERE ARE 867,000 WAYS OF INTERPRETING POVERTY / LIVING WITHIN YOUR MEANS. RESEARCH THE TOPIC.

16. THANK YOUR HIGHER POWER FOR THE INVISIBLE RICHES IN LIFE, NOT THE ONES THAT CAN BE BOUGHT.

LINDA MARY MONTANO
21 MAY 2011
THE ART/LIFE INSTITUTE
TRANSFIGURATION HOSPITAL
http://lindamarymontano.blogspot.com
GOOGLE: LINDA MARY MONTANO

An Artist Residency in Motherhood Manifesto (2012)

Lenka Clayton

<u>Artist's Statement</u>

In common with all new parents, the birth of my first child in April 2011 changed many things in my life. One of those changes has been the way I and others think about my career as an artist. I find now that many aspects of the professional art world are closed to artists with families. Most prestigious artist residencies for example specifically exclude families from attending. Despite a legacy of public artist/parents it still seems to be a commonly held belief that being an engaged mother and serious artist are mutually exclusive endeavors. I don't believe or want to perpetrate this. I like to imagine the two roles not as competing directions but to view them, force them gently if necessary, to inform one another.

I will undergo this self-imposed artist residency in order to fully experience and explore the fragmented focus, nap-length studio time, limited movement and resources and general upheaval that parenthood brings and allow it to shape the direction of my work, rather than try to work "despite it".

This website will document my attempts.
http://www.artistresidencyinmotherhood.com

Let's see.

L.C. September 2012

MANIFESTA (2013)

SILVIA ZIRANEK

ART
ART!
ART?.............. ART!!!
MORE........
MORE ART, MORE ARTISTS, MORE MEANS, MORE WAYS, MORE GOOD,
MORE LIFE
MORE QUALITY THROUGH FEMALE QUANTITY
MORE NOW
MAKE ART NOW
MAKE GOOD ART
MAKE GOOD ART NOW
MAKE MORE ART NOW
MAKE MORE GOOD ART OURS NOW
MAKE OUR ART
MAKE NOW ART
DO THE MAKING, DO THE MATHS, DO THE DO
DID IT, AM DOING IT, SHALL DO, SHALL HOPE TO DO TO BE
BE THE DO, BE THE DOING, BE THE ART, BE THE NOW, BE THE MAKE
JUST BE
JUST BEING
JUST ART
JUST OUR ART
JUST US
JUST NOW
BE NOW
ART NOW
ART...
ART!

Manifesto for the Gynecene
Sketch of a New Geological Era (2015)

Alexandra Pirici and Raluca Voinea

Introduction

At this point in time we believe a radical change in politics and the world socio-economic system is needed in order to achieve a new balanced ecology and this radical change should start with a shifting of agency: we ask for the main agency to be shifted to the feminine principle – which we do not understand as excluding masculinity but as referring to a history of incorporating it and mobilizing it in a different way than the traditional patriarchal mobilization for violence: an emphasis on complementarity rather than antagonism, on resolutions of peace rather than militarism, on efforts directed towards construction, care and emancipatory exploration rather than destruction.

We declare the imperative necessity for **a new geological era** to be commenced, before the Anthropocene is even officially admitted on that scale (it might be that by the time it gets fully acknowledged, it will be too late). Rather than continue to contemplate our annihilation, contributing to it or declaring hopelessness in front of it, we should at least try another approach – and this approach has to exclude patriarchy in all its expressions and institutionalized forms of violence: domination, exploitation, slavery, colonialism, profit, exclusion, monarchy, oligarchy, mafia, religious wars.

The Gynecene: This new geological era can be thought of as the **Gynecene**. Understanding the term does not mean thinking of a "women's world" which excludes virility but as a world which mobilizes it towards humanist and animist goals rather than oppressive, violent and colonial enterprises. We see the feminine as equivalent not to a gender but to a condition, not a "natural" condition but a cultural one. The feminine is the first stage towards a transgressive humanism and the Gynecene is the first global and simultaneous transfer of the feminine imprint onto the physical and political strata (deeply connected as they are today) of the Earth.

Moreover, trying to imagine a future ecology for the whole planetary assemblage, not only a future for the human race, we support the idea that any desirable mode of existence connected / integrated into nature-culture or constituted of equally important organic and inorganic life-forms (including an animistic perspective) cannot be separated from the human subject's struggle to overcome oppression based on gender, race and class within the species. Insofar as we cannot speak of "man" – the human species – as a unity, we have to support these struggles as interconnected and fight them simultaneously, we need to imagine and constantly discuss the connections and similarities as well as the contradictions arising.

43

Preliminary Principles:

1. The female body **has to** cease functioning as a battlefield. The brutal reality of the female condition in general is its intrinsic physical vulnerability. Whatever soft power, it cannot be backed by hard power as usual. We support an empowering of women that is founded on a desired change of paradigm, where weakness is understood and respected as a valuable condition in itself, and at the same time on the possibility, accepted and de-tabooed, of technological transformations of the human body towards hybrid forms such as the cyborg. We are fighting the normalized body and the ideologies that marginalize "imperfections of" or "deviations from" this norm. We support preservation of difference as a choice but without an obligation of difference, feminism as a fight for real freedom of choice. We believe in the possibility of infinitely expanding and shifting bodily configurations and consciousness. As our physical and chemical limits also limit our perceptions and our experiencing of the world, we embrace transhumanism or expanded humanism as a possible solution to the challenge of belonging to the human race.

2. Only a radical left can oppose a growing radical right and recover the territory that remains to the forces of reaction. Only a strong belief – **with universal ambitions** – in equality of races and gender, in equal rights for women, queers, the poor and the disenfranchised, in negotiation with animal rights and the rights of inorganic entities – **all linked together** – can stand against and oppose an expansive and interconnected politics of exclusion, capitalist exploitation, religious fundamentalism, racism, sexism and brutal anthropocentrism.

3. A radical left has to oppose physical violence in conjunction with the opposition to economic or symbolic violence. Jobs in the arms industry or trade are feeding several families while destroying thousands others. Domestic violence is not depending on the degree of wealth or education. Hunting for pleasure or destroying natural and cultural monuments that are part of humanity's patrimony are not class-related. Therefore the new, truly radical left has to rebuild itself on a different type of revolution, which takes us beyond the traditional class antagonisms and can face the neo-tribal reality of today in which violence breeds violence, justice is used as a tool for revenge and critique of power is increasingly powerless. While the world peace has been a goal of many states, attempted at through different international treaties, it has always failed into more arming and lately it has completely degenerated into the obsession of security, enforced through the militarization of the police force and the increasing surveillance of every aspect of our existence. Any form of justice in a future sustainable society has to be imagined and exercised in another realm than that of retaliation, deprivation of basic human rights and brutality.

4. We consider the analysis of capitalism and its catastrophic consequences is complete and time has come to move on. Any time spent on "revealing" the more subtle or more flagrant inconsistencies of this system's adepts is a time lost in achieving a better present and future. We must spare energy and unite forces in providing for this better future as of now. "We have more important things to do than to try to get you to come around. You will come around when you have to, because you need us more than we need you. . . ." (Shulamith Firestone)

Also, capitalism in itself cannot be extracted and separated from discussions around all conservative politics and conservative views, as we have understood that neoliberalism is not truly liberal but a rather paradoxical mix of advocacy for economic "freedom" and racist, sexist and conservative extrapolations of nuclear family/dynasty values. It is not an external, malignant, alien entity but a set of historic conditions and current practices, which instead of introjecting we have to learn how to live without.

5. In order to achieve a truly pluralistic society where possibilities can be enacted, we support the universalism of basic human rights as a common ground for a broader, inter-species and inter-objective politics of inclusion and true respect for difference. The Earth is no longer a big and ungraspable planet, but a shared living room (a shrinking one, moreover) in which we have to coexist by negotiating and conciliating our different views and practices, while recognizing we can only do that through a reciprocal process and towards the un-negotiable goal of equality of gender, race, class and sexual orientation, with no second class citizens. Also, the instrumentalisation and use by double standards of the concept of "freedom" is by no means a reason to abandon it altogether, but a reminder that we must constantly fight for it.

6. Natural resources are a common good. Everyone should have equal access to them. Economic equality should be the basis of society and therefore we strongly support the universal basic income. Equal and free access to healthcare, lodging, education and to culture should be granted for everyone, at any time of their life.

Communities should be self-governed, in the interest of the communities (as well as of all the individuals that are part of them). Everyone should have the right of free movement, in the spirit of a universal citizenship. We also support a certain ambition to overcome the imperative to work through technological advancement (see point 8).

7. Pluralism is possible only on the ground of a universal, secular frame which allows for a certain relativisation of belief. We can only respect and support religion that is compatible, in its majoritarian practices and interpretations, with the right to a secular education (which can guarantee the least freedom of choice in matters of religion), that embraces equal rights for women, queers and non-believers and a politics of freedom rather than a politics of submission and interdiction, apart from protecting basic human rights. We can only respect and support religion that is based on a freedom of experimenting and observing, not on a prescriptive set of rules, interdictions and punishments proclaimed by a patriarchal, self-asserted authority perfectly mimicking the structure of a monarchy or a dictatorship. Providing easy and simple answers for the complexity of human existence might fake the offering of a "meaning" and help some survive, but it will never help us evolve.

8. We also believe the emancipatory use of sustainable technology has to play an important part in any future ecology, including the protection and preservation of "nature", just as much as a needed change in our position towards nature and its exclusive understanding as resource for endless consumption. Our ability to negotiate between the two will be of crucial importance for constructing a future ecology. Development of technology must be pursued in agreement with the respect for nature and its limits and it must not be submitted to private interests or corporate profit. Technology is a cultural asset and together with the rest of culture, it must be made public, open and free, put to the benefit of emancipating humanity while not destroying everything else around it.

Provisional conclusion:
We declare the beauty of the world has to be enriched by a new beauty: the beauty of kindess. Instead of directly escaping into the dream of a still far-fetched machinic future that could masterfully end the limited perspective of our species or into the conservative retreat to a past which is impossible and not desirable to bring back to life, we beleive the Gynecene can be the gateway to a true pluratistic and expanded humanism, one which is compatible with machinic desires and existing forms of life, which is inhuman in its break with human history as much as it is human in its enactment of our current possibilities. We believe the endless quest for meaning can be momentarily satisfied by recognizing each other as individual constants in a collective, fragile, subjective time, facing the vastness of our cosmic surroundings and bound by imagining together our future extnesions. It is this togetherness, in its most abstract form that should be capable of creating a sense of unity across our seemingly incompatible histories and a toutal break with History, after extracting its most emancipatory moments, and that could propel us from the "Man" made Anthropocene to the true collective existence of the Gynecene.

Alexandra Pirici and Raluca Voinea
January 2015, Bucharest and Bologna.

Feminist (Art) Institution : CODE OF PRACTICE

This **Code of Practice** is one of the outputs of a seminar held in spring as part of the tranzit.cz 2017 programme. The seminar examined the possible forms of organisations and collectives that wish to be seen as feminist.

A feminist art institution regards feminist thinking to be an important resource, an inspiration, and one of the underlying bases of its programme and operations. Such an institution is inspired by the history of feminist organisation and by feminist reflections upon power, work, relationships, and forms of oppression.

1. A feminist art institution is (self)-critical. It subjects its structure and programme to review in order to reflect changing social conditions. It recognises that it cannot be separated from the social context, and selects its methods of social engagement accordingly. A feminist art institution seeks to develop new types of institutional environment. It redefines what it means to be a public institution and embraces groups that are otherwise marginalised or discriminated against within the concept of public. It deems art (hence culture) to be a universally shared asset (the commons), to which everyone has an inalienable right.

Feminist art institutions are steadfastly opposed to all manifestations of intolerance, e.g. racism, homophobia or sexism. They formulate strategies for dealing with such situations should they arise.

Feminist art institutions champion the viewpoint of the oppressed, and this is reflected in their programme, their relationship with the public, and their own internal organisation.

2. The ethics of its own internal operations are as important to a feminist art institution as the programme by which it presents itself to the public. On the one hand, it works towards the objectives it wishes to see enshrined in society, and on the other ensures that those who work for it are happy and feel that their opinion counts. An organisational structure must be created that is capable of developing a meaningful programme while taking into account the needs of those who are part of it.

A feminist art institution is based on the mutual respect of those who work in it. The quality of their relationships, irrespective of what position they occupy, is considered to be of equal importance as the quality of the programme.

The operations of a feminist art institution are the outcome of collective discussion and decision-making, and not a 'one wo/man show'. The distribution of power is clearly articulated. It is subject to debate on the part of all interested parties and can be changed.

3. A feminist art institution is based on a feminist understanding of work. It is inspired by the importance feminist theory attributes to care (for children, the elderly, sick and handicapped) and other activities that cannot be monetised but are crucial for the wellbeing of society. One of the aims of a feminist art institution is to raise the profile of activities that are essential to the existence of any organisation yet are taken for granted and financially unremunerated. Different types of care (and art can be deemed a type of care) are of crucial concern to a feminist art institution.

A feminist art institution is receptive to caregivers and adapts its programme so that they are able to participate.

Example: *It is barrier-free, offers childminding services and the appropriate space, organises its events at times that suit parents with children, and ensures its events are accessible to people with physical or mental health issues.*

A feminist art institution is receptive to those of its workers who have responsibilities as carers. It makes every attempt to create a working environment that includes space for care activities.

Example: *Employees have the opportunity to work from home. It offers childminding services during working hours. It factors in the presence of small children on its premises.*

The work of production managers, accountants and all those who contribute to the upkeep and maintenance of the institution is recognised and respected.

Example: *A feminist art institution's programme lists all those involved. There is no difference between the fee paid production managers and curators.*

A feminist art institution pays a fee to everyone who participates directly in its running or programme. (An exception to this rule involves institutions operating on a DIY basis where nobody is paid.) Gender has no influence on the level of the fee whatsoever.

4. A feminist art institution takes it as an article of faith that contemporary society is patriarchal, as is the contemporary art world. The aim of the institution is to participate in the struggle to change this situation.

A feminist art institution therefore promotes quotas as a temporary solution to gender imbalance and discrimination.

A feminist art institution promotes a 50% minimum representation of women in its annual programme, whether this involve exhibitions, festivals, conferences or panel discussions.

At least 50% of all managerial, creative and other positions of responsibility are occupied by women in a feminist (art) institution.

A feminist art institution refuses to abide by the unwritten criteria of the culture industry as we know it today. The art world is based on a system of competition, in which only those who demonstrate the requisite endurance, ambition, strength, assertiveness succeed. A feminist art institution advocates other values and virtues. It takes into account human weakness, frailty and fatigue, and prioritises human relationships over 'performance'. It sets itself different rules within the framework of its possibilities.

Representatives of Prague Art Institutions.

The following art institutions have declared themselves bound by this Code of Practice: Artwall, Display, etc. gallery, INI Project, Jindrich Chalupecky Society, tranzit.cz, Institute of Anxiety, Kapitál.

n i i c h e g o d e l a t (2017 - 2021)

n i i c h e g o d e l a t (Social Research Institute, SRI for doing nothing) is a social movement that stands for post-labor society. The n i i c h e g o d e l a t raises questions of the emancipation of workers from alienated labor, and of the unemployed from social stigmatization and resurrects the utopian tradition of striving to a future world without work.

The current order requires everyone to work more, to buy more, to be more active, more communicative, more creative, more extraordinary, more liquid – and all in order to sell us everything more expensively, to put a new brick in its foundation and to intensify our alienation from reality. In this situation – to stop, to break down, to refuse to do anything becomes a common and explainable reaction. But the one who does not produce – the one who does nothing, procrastinates – is an asshole, a loser, an outcast thrown out of the orbit of social life and even less able to change anything in the existing order. The desire to "do nothing" is a forbidden desire, and therefore it is hidden, suppressed, rejected.

We honestly admit to ourselves that our present desire is to do nothing.
We honestly admit to ourselves that we doubt. And we see that we are many.

The main goal of the Research Institute is to consider "doing nothing" and its other varieties (procrastination, passivity, apathy, idleness, etc.) are a public phenomenon requiring comprehensive study, both theoretical and practical. An important aspect of the Institute's activity is the therapy of "procrastinators" and "idlers", whose condition in fact turns out to be "painful and disfigured".

MAY 1 2018 (https://www.youtube.com/watch?v=wdXsXfze5Lc&t=26s)

On May 1, the n i i c h e g o d e l a t (SRI for doing nothing) went out to the annual demonstration in the centre of Saint Petersburg for solidarity with the working people and parasites.

Our slogans and catchwords on LABOUR DAY:
     What to do? Do nothing.
     World without work.
     Parasites of all countries unite.
     Without labor.
     You can't put a job into mouth – the Institute is for Basic Income!
     A freelancer is also a person.
     Down with dictatorship of larks.
     I'm tired of trying to sell myself to other hands.
     Don't get out of bed for any mister.

Come on, procrastination – capitalism will die!
Come on, procrastination – capitalism awaits elimination!
I have a right for a crisis.
Marx! Sex! May! The world without labor will come one day!
Working day, working night! Pay me for raising my child!

ZOMBIE

For a long time researchers of SRI for doing nothing have been trying to invent
a vaccine against work. As a result of accident a post-labor virus has been
created. This virus has turned all the researchers of the Institute into zombies
and at last set them free from their work.

Project «NIIK - pik» Picnic,

Kanonersky Island Environmental Biennale 2 (July 2017)
Installation, performance.
A picnic as interface of communication between nature and human.
This project of n i i c h e g o d e l a t is an attempt to think about ecology in a
new way.
We insist that direct interaction between human and nature is not possible.
Attempts to save the planet fail and give only false moral comfort. We propose
to create a new interface between the human and the natural using a strategy
of double estrangement. Being alienated from our own humanity, we liberate
nature from natural, and therefore from a subordinate position. Destroying the
false dichotomy between "the artificial" and "the natural", we will try to create a
new symbiotic-aesthetic landscape, an eco-system of the 21st century, where
humans as a species and polyethylene, sand, water, moss, broken trees,
orange peels, insects, stones, concrete blocks will try to coexist together.

Caution, decomposition!

An experimental design of the ecology of n i i c h e g o d e l a t
{over dose decompose}.
Hypothesis: to protect the environment from harmful human activity, it is
necessary to do nothing. Outside of passivity, the body inevitably begins to
rot, the remains that have not undergone rotting petrify. Then the question is in
time. We can begin the process — how much can it be shown within the event?
How is the intention expressed without action? Site preparation, marking, public
statement, warning signs, volunteers, journalists, MES?

Practice of small movements.

A researcher of the Institute, Marina Russkih, offers a practice of small
movements as an experimental method of doing nothing which allows you to
overcome the enslaving rationale of capitalistic oppression. Let yourself be slow.
Feel the touch of air against the back of your palm. Hang inbetween.

Age riot (video) https://www.youtube.com/watch?v=fXE68EBIJ_o
Marina Russkih, a researcher of n i i c h e g o d e l a t, tries to answer the question "what to do?" – or reflections of a young pensioner on the ruins of a crystal palace from a beautiful future.
What does the young pensioner have in common with young artists?
Like young artists, the young pensioner stands at a crossroads; both of them are experiencing a feeling of some uncertainty, perhaps even fear, and are trying to find answers to the questions:
Where to go? How to live further? What to do?

«Yes, I am 57 and I don't feel comfortable speaking about this because I feel awkward. It's odd but it's awkward to be 57 years old. That's why people don't usually talk about their age too much. As for me, in my late fifties, I am young curator and young artist. But when I look for any residencies or internships, I always encounter those restrictions: everywhere they only welcome really young artists and curators up to 35 years. And when I ask myself– "Who am I", "Where am I", "What am I" – I don't have any answer! At the same time, I declare my own small and personal riot against ageism and when I encounter this question: "What should I do?" – now I have an answer: "Dance. And read Ranciere."»

Last rave (video installation) https://www.youtube.com/watch?v=oRdtsoQanAY&t=170s
Nadya Ishkinyaeva, a researcher of n i i c h e g o d e l a t, tries to pretend what will be rest in the future.
It, the n i i c h e g o d e l a t, is always a break. All participants undertake procedures in the water. Three pairs of female legs, like three graces, roll across the ceiling. Symbolic paradise and the specter of a serene future, where no one works and everyone is resting. New people have achieved universal equality and justice, they only have to be active participants in the social movement «to do nothing». New people are there, and we are here – we look through the water for a brighter future. Who are we if they are there, and we are here? Are we old people? Are we ordinary people? Are we people of the present? Are we stones at the bottom of the pool?

n i i c h e g o d e l a t for (s)lot "round dance of uncertainty":
AliStopcran is an online shop, with elusive objects of desire, wild descriptions and forever slamming opportunities.
During the session and operation of the store, (s) lots will be offered, one of which will be selected in a contingent way (roll of dice) and presented to the viewer / consumer of the content.
AliStopkran's online store is full of elusive desires, crazy descriptions and eternal possibilities of punching.

During the store's session / work, advertising spots will be provided, one of which will be selected by a temporary method (dice) and presented to the viewer / consumer of the content:

AliStopkran's online store is full of intense passions, crazy descriptions and, possibly, verwelkomd (very welcome) ribs.
During the session / store operation, a place for advertising will be provided, one of which will be selected in a preliminary format (dice) and submitted to the competition:

AliStopkran's repository is full of lust, crazy ideas, and possibly verwelkomd ribs.
During the course / store, a place for advertising will be provided, one of which will be selected in a short period of time (dice) and shown on joo:

AliStopkran's data warehouse is full of passions, jokes, and possibly nervous jokes.
During the reading / showroom, a space will be created which will be selected for a short time (dice) and displayed in the zoo:

Slots:
(s) lot of temporal synchronization (deadlines, apparatus for regulating collectivity). Temporal violence *n* (work "for uncle") and temporal emancipation (common cause). Queer temporality.
(s) lot of attention modes, about dispersion and concentration (scanner, achieving success, with the side effect of burnout / combustion of thinking machines), about post attention (bodily attention, attention in the stream, surfing).
(s) lot of uncertainty ("I just look"; the uncertainty immediately after passing the exam / work and until the result is obtained) about the environment of opportunities and frustration that forms subjectivity.
(s) lot gate of binarity.
(s) lot of missed desires and expectations / slot of missed opportunities.
(s) lot of superposition (whether the action gave a result and whether it is the result of an action that could have occurred or not, I / we are the Schrödinger / Heisenberg cat).
(s) lot "Terminator — neither fish nor meat". Slot of freedom from choice.
(s) lot of obsessive conditions

Additional features of the store environment:
Empty / beaten (s) lot
Fake (s) lots>
(s) lot does not meet expectations
During preparation, all the slots may change or disappear.

Manifesto of the Utopian Unemployment Union (2017)

Artists and Refugees Unite!

We call out to you courageous creatures without jobs, visas and or status, Mothers and children, Lions, Eagles and Partridges, Winged deer, Fish, and Algae and Sea Wheat and all microorganisms, witnesses of migrants drowned on their way to Europe and to the destroyed houses and the suffering people from wars, in a word, all lives, that completed their sorrowful circle now embodied as nomadic artists. You are the new people, born from globalism, who have speed up the circulation of their cells to an impossible degree. The collective world soul is in all of us. In us dwells the soul of the great free spirits, and also the smallest leech. The strands of cosmic consciousness are interwoven in us and we remember everything, everything, everything and we relive every life over again within ourselves.

> – Whose side are you on? The masters of culture? was asked long ago by Maxim Gorky.
> – Artists are on the side of the weak, said Gluklya and Tsaplya.
> – Where is equality, I asked the birds and they flew far away.
> – Where is equality, I asked the feminists. – There is equality, but not sameness, they said.
> – Where is equality, I asked the art teacher with degrees from three different European institutions – There is no equality, he said, and that in itself is equality.

But there is equality between Refugee and Artist! We have found it! Imagine Schiphol Airport becoming a Theatre of the Utopian Union of Unemployed People!

All new arrivals in the European Union and residents together will be actors of their own play, the play which is training mussels on the sense of true equality and justice. The European Citizenship will be judged according to the Demands of the New Theatre:

- Empathy
- Compassion and Solidarity
- Overcoming fears
- Forgiving

•Subversive Humour
•Devotion to Friends
•Sense of Entire Beauty
•Creation

Capability to reinvent yourself and move further!
These are the new demands for issuing a visa to the e world civic theatre: the start of a new society.

The new revolution will come!

We need it in order to stop the frightful course of impossible alienation and stop the destruction of the planet by means of the new attainments of equality.

There is no other way for us!

And here we are out in the street.

We do not agree that the streets where we used to shape our society should be given away. The street should be of the people. Let's subvert the ossified order of things. Down with idiotic expensive shops! Down with the elite order of shiny trinkets that bring happiness to nobody! Down with gentrification and the brazen despotism of developers!

Architects! Do not submit! Turn down such projects! Artists! Writers! Musicians! Ecologists! Philosophers! For the sake of Refugees and all creatures: join the Utopian Unemployment Union!

Join the Potato Eaters party for resistance, the Monster party for overcoming of fears, the Language of Fragility party to express your feelings, the Recycling Prison party to overhaul the system and, the Spirit of History party to bring new life to the Revolution!

Gluklya / Natalia Pershina-Yakimanskaya

We are not surprised.
We are artists, arts administrators, assistants, curators, directors, editors, educators, gallerists, interns, scholars, students, writers, and more—workers of the art world—and we have been groped, undermined, harassed, infantilized, scorned, threatened, and intimidated by those in positions of power who control access to resources and opportunities. We have held our tongues, threatened by power wielded over us and promises of institutional access and career advancement.

We are **not surprised** when curators offer exhibitions or support in exchange for sexual favors. We are **not surprised** when gallerists romanticize, minimize, and hide sexually abusive behavior by artists they represent. We are **not surprised** when a meeting with a collector or a potential patron becomes a sexual proposition. We are **not surprised** when we are retaliated against for not complying. We are **not surprised** when Knight Landesman gropes us in the art fair booth while promising he'll help us with our career. **Abuse of power comes as no surprise.**

This open letter stems from a group discussion about sexual harassment within our field, following the recent revelation of Knight Landesman's sexual misconduct. The conversation has branched out further and internationally. Harder work to advance equity is often expected of and performed by women of color, trans, and gender nonconforming people. Our efficacy relies on taking this intersection very seriously and not excluding other corroborating factors that contribute to bias, exclusion, and abuse. These additional factors include, but are not limited to, race, gender identity, sexual identity, ability, religion, class, political position, economic and immigration status. There is an urgent need to share our accounts of widespread sexism, unequal and inappropriate treatment, harassment and sexual misconduct, which we experience regularly, broadly, and acutely.

Many institutions and individuals with power in the art world espouse the rhetoric of feminism and equity in theory, often financially benefitting from these flimsy claims of progressive politics, while preserving oppressive and harmful sexist norms in practice. Those in power ignore, excuse, or commit everyday instances of harassment and degradation, creating an environment of acceptance of and complicity in many more serious, illegal abuses of power.

The resignation of one publisher from one high-profile magazine does not solve the larger, more insidious problem: an art world that upholds inherited power structures at the cost of ethical behavior. Similar abuses occur frequently and on a large scale within this industry. We have been silenced, ostracized, pathologized, dismissed as "overreacting," and threatened when we have tried to expose sexually and emotionally abusive behavior.

We will be silenced no longer.

We will denounce those who would continue to exploit, silence, and dismiss us. Your actions will no longer be a secret, whispered amongst us for fear of ostracization, professional shunning, and recrimination. Where we see the abuse of power, we resolve to speak out, to demand that institutions and individuals address our concerns seriously, and to bring these incidents to light regardless of the perpetrator's gender.

We will no longer ignore the condescending remarks, the wayward hands on our bodies, the threats and intimidations thinly veiled as flirtation, or the silence from ambitious colleagues. We will not tolerate being shamed or disbelieved, and we will not tolerate the recrimination that comes with speaking out. We will not join "task forces" to solve a problem that is perpetrated upon us. We provide a definition of sexual harassment, for those who may feel powerless so that they may point to a document that supports a safe work environment for all.

We, the undersigned—those who have experienced abuse and those standing in solidarity with them—call upon art institutions, boards, and peers to consider their role in the perpetuation of different levels of sexual inequity and abuse, and how they plan to handle these issues in the future.

We are too many, now, to be silenced or ignored.

With all we have experienced and witnessed,
this letter should come as **no surprise**.

This letter is dedicated to the memory of feminist art historian Linda Nochlin (1931-2017), whose activism, spirit, and pioneering writings have been an inspiration for our work.

#NOTSURPRISED
This letter is the first public step. We will continue to address and act upon these issues as part of a larger process, building the next steps through the feedback we receive.

We Propose

Declaration of Commitment to Feminist Practices in Art

Nosotras Propemos / Permanent Assembly of Women Art Workers

We propose

Given increased awareness of forms of sexual harassment in the art world, we—artists, curators, researchers, writers, gallerists, art workers—state our commitment to feminist practices. This document, which we invite you to sign, is intended to create awareness of patriarchal practices that shape the exercise of power in the art world. The open letter «We Are Not Surprised» issued a «call upon art institutions, boards, and peers to consider their role in the perpetuation of different levels of sexual inequity and abuse, and how they plan to handle these issues in the future». In this statement of commitment to feminist practices, we attempt to expand awareness of the patriarchal and sexist behavior pervasive in the art world, behavior that regulates how we position ourselves. While this statement addresses, first, the historical exclusion and devaluation of women artists, its proposals can be embraced by women, men, or those with non-normative identities. It sets out to act as a suggested guide to personal and institutional practices.

Concerning the structure of the art world

1. We demand equal representation in the art world (strategically 50% instead of the current 20%): the collections of museums and other cultural institutions, as well as in private collections; group shows; awards and distinctions (parity in the number of awards and distinctions given, and jury members); art fairs; representations at international events such as biennials; reproductions of works in books and catalogs; covers of magazines and journals; and number of artists represented by art galleries. Parity should be the guideline in all of the arts (in the programming of concerts and works in the performing arts, and in literature). We will make visible and dismantle the unequal distribution of funding, resources, and income (between different genders, between «centers» and «peripheries,» between different social sectors).

2. We will work for parity in the top-level positions at the artistic, educational, and cultural institutions that determine and enact policies in the visual arts. In Argentina, there are few female museum directors; the most powerful positions at art institutions are mainly held by men. Women generally hold mid-level jobs, performing «feminine» tasks linked to the patrimonial sphere (restoration, cataloging, conservation) or at the head of initiatives in

education; if they do hold top-level jobs, it is usually at museums considered "minor" in relation to the "centers" of the arts (decorative art museums, museums of fashion design). The privileged speakers on panels or at roundtables are mostly men, and «stars» of the art world are overwhelmingly male. In organizations (not only at commercial venues, but also at self-run and supposedly horizontal spaces like assemblies and art projects), we will make ourselves visible and avoid to be placed only in the traditional roles of secretary, administrative assistant, press officer, while men are assigned creative and leadership tasks. We will attempt to work solely with those who feel that everyone is capable of acting and of learning.

3. We will be aware that heterosexual men are not the only ones to engage in patriarchal behavior: women can be extremely patriarchal when they act in an authoritarian manner and mistreat others. The gay culture can also be patriarchal. We will strengthen our alliance with "locas" and the queer community in order to dismantle gay misogyny. We will recognize male colleagues that follow feminist perspectives in their practices.

4. We will analyze the position of women and other feminized bodies in issues of race, social class, age, geography, sexual orientation, gender identity, and other differential vectors, and actively work to subvert the overwhelming discriminatory and excluding tendency in the art world that favors white, middle or upper class, young, and well-connected artists. We will support research and greater visibility of women artist with different social backgrounds and cultures. We will point out and analyze the exclusion of mid-career women artists and the recent and growing phenomenon of late recognition of female artists, which the press has called, in dismissive and discriminatory tone, «granny recognition».

Concerning behaviors in the art world

5. We will not fall into the trap of the personal accusation («She is difficult»): institutions and powerful figures always want to convince us that asking for our due, setting boundaries, fighting for the dignity of our work, means that we are uppity and out of line, or outright «crazy,» «hysterical,» or «problematic.»

6. Whenever we are about to criticize, aloud or otherwise, another woman, we will stop to consider whether we are engaging in a learned form of hatred. Misogyny is ingrained in the collective unconscious, and we have to take it apart within ourselves. When in doubt, we will ask ourselves what would happen if a man were doing the thing we are criticizing.

7. We will avoid expending too much energy supporting the careers of our male colleagues rather than those of our female colleagues. We will cultivate respectful and egalitarian working relationships with the men in our milieu without enabling micro acts of sexism.

8. When we have the chance to help another woman gain confidence in herself, we will. If a woman helps us gain confidence, we will recognize it and thank her.

9.   We will avoid being discredited by acts of paternalism and demand revision of
      the language used by our male colleagues to neutralize our arguments and to
      impose their own. We will seek to keep our male colleagues from explaining to
      and correcting us (mansplaining) on the assumption that we know little about
      a given subject.
10.   We will not be intimidated by volume or tone of voice, or by the physical
      stature, of our male interlocutors. None of that makes them right.
11.   We will not feel ashamed of the issues we are interested or involved in: shame
      is one of the patriarchy's strategies to hinder research on certain topics.
12.   We will explicitly oppose strategies of power and those who engage in them
      every time we come across them.
13.   We will listen to each other and share experiences, because the personal is
      always political. We will promote friendship between women. We counter
      corporative sexism with solidarity between women (sorority).

Concerning the artistic career and creativity

14.   We will create as much as we can. We will not be afraid to be ambitious.
      Creating more is a way to work for gender equality.
15.   We will identify and ward off the plundering of our artistic ideas and practices,
      which often go unnoticed when produced or enacted by women only to gain
      notoriety when produced or enacted by men. We will draw public attention
      to that when it happens. We have noticed that qualities associated with
      "feminine" art are considered minor, kitsch, amateurish, childish, or ridiculous
      in the work of women artists but valued if in the work of men.
16.   We will challenge the definition of «artistic career» as full-time dedication
      to the production of work to commercial ends. As women, we know that our
      ability to work is often conditioned by motherhood and by the work of caring
      for our families and their needs—material and emotional. We will uphold
      careers that include interruptions as a specific value in our practices. We will
      fight for the equal distribution of domestic work and care (including emotional
      support) and question how naturally those tasks are imposed to us and how
      naturally we embrace them.
17.   We reject the concept of "the genius," of the master artist, and of the canon of
      «good art» regulated by patriarchal parameters.
18.   We will cast off the «expert eye» capable of discerning, almost mystically,
      artistic quality.

Concerning artistic feminism and feminist art history

19.   We will not avoid identifying ourselves as feminist artists or as feminist art
      historians when our practices encompass feminist art, politics, and activism.
      We will take pride in calling our work feminist insofar as it questions the
      dominant hetero-patriarchal system.

20. We will question the stereotyped images of «women» according to patriarchal discourses. We will build our own categories.
21. We will study the work of women artists, researchers, and theorists; we will heed their legacies; we will reexamine the power over us exercised by patriarchal genealogies; we will value women's knowledge.
22. We will reexamine what and whom we cite and how we have internalized patriarchal thinking and principles of authority in our practices.
23. We will analyze the patriarchal language that dominates the construction of art history (terms like genius, manifesto, teacher) to develop another perspective, other stories and other art histories.
24. We demand that female authors of art history and theory be included in academic curricula.
25. We will mention female colleagues and their work in conversations with curators, collectors, gallerists, and other agents in the art field. We will attend lectures, read interviews, and study work pertinent to women artists—an effective way to criticize the dominant patriarchal genealogies.
26. We will never name female artists as the wives or partners of male artists, linking them solely to male genealogies. We will avoid using the last name of the male member of the couple and the first name of the female member (e.g. Frida and Diego Rivera). Art history has been built on the marginalization of women in artist couples and in the relationships between male masters and female disciples. We will underscore women's independent identities, trajectories, and the place they occupy in the map of creativity.
27. We will make visible and condemn the power systems that belittle the work of women artists on the assumption that they have gained legitimacy in exchange for sexual favors.
28. We will attend women's meetings and conferences and propose sessions on art and feminism. We will speak out in order to compare women's situation in the arts and in other spheres of creation and knowledge.
29. We will pay attention to and learn from the collective, participatory, collaborative, and horizontal nature of feminism in history and its relationship to other subaltern, discredited, and oppressed forms of cultural expression
30. We will work so that the claims for recognition of women artists not recognized during their lifetimes or at the peaks of their productivity is not a passing trend.
31. We will support creation, knowledge, and circulation of collaborative, participatory, and community art, outside the traditionally elitist art field.
32. We will uphold modes of perception based on inclusiveness, on affect, and on equality as opposed to a logic of exclusion and individualism, of patriarchal values that dominate both society and the art world.
33. We will publicly point out that the exclusion of the work of women artists entails systemic and systematic censorship of our sensibilities, of our poetics and forms of knowledge. That silencing means that viewers have access only to male forms of seeing and being in the world.

Concerning the inclusive nature of this statement

34. We will fight to make the male art community and the art community in general open to different (and equally important) sensibilities.
35. We understand, and encourage our male colleagues to understand, that men as well as women and everybody in between can make this commitment. The principles of fairness and respect must be applied, preached, and upheld by all.
36. We believe that feminism is connected to awareness of discrimination and oppression not only of women, but of all other individuals dismissed for reasons of class, race, gender identity, or sexual orientation: feminism is an emancipatory dialectical moment for everyone.
37. We will not be accomplices to any form of sexist violence, from the most visible to the most subtle and imperceptible. We will look for effective non-punitive, solutions: we will protect ourselves and protect our spaces. We will be there for each other.

The impetus for this proposal was the unexpected and premature death of Argentine artist Graciela Sacco, who doggedly combated many of the behaviors described here.

On November 7, 2017, we founded the Permanent Assembly of Art Workers to promote feminist practices.

We are a transnational coalition of feminists, awake to our positioning as "Others" within the patriarchy; awake to our exclusion from unmarked norm(s) PEGGY PHELAN; awake to our emergence from a history of subjugation, subordination, and colonization; mindful of our privileges (if any) art and architectural historians, interrogating space and representation, thinking critically about cultural/social production, and resisting monolithic disciplinary identities theorists, with the unique responsibility to dismantle and disrupt the canons of our fields and disciplines and practitioners. who design, build, and intervene in spatial environments MATRIX

We are scholars.
We are researchers, participating in knowledge production and invested in its futures critics, intellectuals, and thinkers dismantling hierarchies of cultural and social production TITHI BATTACHARYA responding to a call for collaboration. learning from each other and building inclusive and diverse communities both inside and outside of our professional lives

We are employees,

moving into and out of a variety of contracts. We are tenured and untenured, with fixed-term or permanent contracts. We are lecturers, adjuncts, graduate students, student employees, research fellows, administrators, staff members, independent scholars, and "spousal" and "diversity" hires

teachers,

challenging learning minds to think critically about the production of space, the representation of individuals/cultures, and the lived environment, and encouraging them to transgress. bELL hOOKS
We value listening as much as we do speaking

activists, and instigators

attuned to the inequities of the spaces in which we do our work and live, advocating and fighting to reshape them, remaining sensitive

gathered on

occupied land.

convening in the occupied territory of the Lenape and Delaware peoples

We are citizens; we are aliens; we are immigrants and emigrants; we are permanent and temporary residents; we are foreign nationals, dual citizens, colonizers, the colonized and formerly colonized, refugees, and children of refugees and diasporas.

moving in and out of relationships to the state and governing institutions. We are enabled and limited to different degrees by our papers SARA AHMED

We are noncompliant bodies of varying dis/ability. sensitive to how we occupy space differently in terms of our gender, race, class, religion, body type, and physical and mental capabilities EMI KOYAMA, COMBAHEE RIVER COLLECTIVE, AUDRE LORDE, ROXANE GAY, JOEL SANDERS, SUSAN STRYKER, BARBARA PENNER, JOS BOYS, WANDA KATJA LIEBERMANN

We demand our right to demand to put forth an impossible demand is to provoke, and to test its validity. We assert our right to demand without offering a road map or a solution. KATHI WEEKS Our goal is to eliminate the need to demand. We want uncontested access to our rights, without having to demand them for to demand is to imagine, to dream, to aspire, to envision. we practice compassion, recognizing humanity and foregrounding the fulfillment of others and our needs We demand from our institutions teacher working conditions are student learning conditions. Education should resist the rules and conditions of capital. Institutions should conceive of themselves as ethical and political agents of change ANGELA DIMITRAKAKI time, for us to transform teaching and for our students to transform learning space, both physical and metaphorical, to act, think, work, experiment, perform, produce, change, and disrupt in, without being penalized or prosecuted stability, as a form of respect for our labor, our care, and our rigor; job precarity is immoral and critical representation. against tokenism and, for underrepresented or overlooked groups, offering a seat at any institutional "table," not just when diversity committees are due We ask our colleagues to become our accomplices, to share in the risk of creating change and in our project of radicalizing education.

to push the boundaries of learning and to build resilient public spaces and open forums on campus and beyond

accomplice (n.): someone who will commit academic crimes with us and share equal risk. "Accomplice" implies a stronger bond than "ally" INDIGENOUS ACTION MEDIA

tenured and permanent positions carry a responsibility to speak truth to power in ways that noncontingent faculty cannot. We ask our colleagues to create platforms for voices that question structural asymmetries and open conversations, and to amplify those voices in campus corridors and administrators' offices

build courage; there is nothing comfortable about structural change. We ask our colleagues to realign priorities, to be brave, to be open to discomfort, to embrace difference of all kinds. This includes, but is not limited to: contracts, career paths, backgrounds, methodologies, race, class, gender, age, ability, ethnicity, and nationality

We are all in this together. We ask our students to fully commit to themselves and to their peers; but we, as educators, also pledge to be radically open,

the work of education is work done together; it is not a solo act but an inherently social one

because the labor of learning is shared labor

collaboration and teamwork can move the project of education forward

mutual support

to embrace messiness and failure, admitting when we do not know or when we lack the expertise to answer

to make space
for exploration and
experimentation,

resisting the "banking model" of education PAULO FREIRE and passive learning whenever possible, teaching in an embodied mode, and mobilizing the greatest breadth of learning modalities

to break down
hierarchies, to recognize modes of resistance and to abstain from reinforcing power differentials to
respect others' identities,

lived experiences, and positions assumed; to enable the tools to speak from different perspectives to the world. We acknowledge noncompliant bodies and minds in our assignments, syllabi, and teaching

and to respect
boundaries. we will practice consent and adopt trauma-informed approaches in difficult conversations. Forms of resistance need support.

For ourselves, we claim the
right to selfcare because

selfcare is radical care AUDRE LORDE; care for the self is care for others. SARA AHMED When necessary, adopt work-to-rule tactics; when necessary, strike. Celebrate our victories at any scale, micro or macro

care is rigor. care should not be the exception to the system PEG RAWES
We need to break down
the double standard that

has pigeonholed women as care-related laborers.

that have alienated, divided, or prevented us from finding subaltern GAYATRI CHAKRAVORTY SPIVAK counterpublics NANCY FRASER and common interests, as well as kept us from connecting across divisions

We reclaim the place of criticality and creative resistance.
Because our cause is to find (and help create) "our people." and thereby transform the institutional structures and the environments within which learning is happening

Because positionalities need to be freed from power structures. support and care are valuable tactics of love; and while love is labor, it isn't payment

We build

connections, conduits, channels, tentacles, ^{DONNA HARAWAY}
and rhizomes, ^{GILLES DELEUZE & FÉLIX GUATTARI}
converting and repurposing structures of power and structures in our teaching

our cause.

resists the increasing power of the for-profit university and its narrowing
constructions of identity and labor. Because education conceived as business puts our students in debt,
in a cycle that perpetuates itself.
We and our students need a more humane, noncapitalist place for our relationships.
The fight for a feminist education is continuous

When? / All the time!
Where? / Everywhere!

Bibliography:
Ahmed, Sara. Living a Feminist Life. Durham, NC: Duke University Press, 2017.
__________. On Being Included: Racism and Diversity in Institutional Life. Durham, NC: Duke University Press, 2012.
__________. Queer Phenomenology: Orientations, Objects, Others. Durham, NC: Duke University Press, 2006.
Bhattacharya, Tithi. Social Reproduction Theory: Remapping Class, Recentering Oppression. London: Pluto Press, 2017.
Boys, Jos, ed. Disability, Space, Architecture: A Reader. London; New York: Routledge, 2017.
Deleuze, Gilles, and Félix Guattari. A Thousand Plateaus: Capitalism and Schizophrenia. London: Athlone Press, 1988.
Dimitrakaki, Angela. Gender, artWork and the Global Imperative: A Materialist Feminist Critique. Manchester: Manchester University Press, 2013.
Fraser, Nancy. "Rethinking the Public Sphere: A Contribution to the Critique of Actually Existing Democracy." Social Text no. 25/26 (1990): 56–80.
Freire, Paulo. Pedagogy of the Oppressed. Translated by Myra Ramos. New York: Herder and Herder, 1970.
Gay, Roxane. Hunger: A Memoir of (My) Body. New York: Harper, 2017.
Haraway, Donna. "A Cyborg Manifesto: Science, Technology, and Socialist-Feminism in the Late Twentieth Century." In Simians, Cyborgs and Women: The Reinvention of Nature, 149–81. New York: Routledge, 1991.
hooks, bell. Teaching to Transgress: Education as the Practice of Freedom. New York: Routledge, 1994.
Indigenous Action Media. "Accomplices Not Allies: Abolishing the Ally Industrial Complex." May 4, 2014. http://www.indigenousaction. org/accomplices-not-allies-abolishing-the-ally-industrial-complex/.
Koyama, Emi. The Transfeminist Manifesto: And Other Essays on Transfeminism. Portland, OR: Emi Koyama, 1999.
Liebermann, Wanda Katja. "The Right to Life in the World: Architecture, Inclusion, and the Americans with Disabilities Act." In Spatializing Politics: Essays on Power and Place, edited by Delia Duong Ba Wendel and Fallon Samuels Aidoo, 273–300. Cambridge, MA: Harvard University Press, 2015.
Lorde, Audre. Sister Outsider: Essays and Speeches. Trumansburg, NY: Crossing Press, 1984.
Matrix. Making Space: Women and the Man-Made Environment. London: Pluto Press, 1984.
Penner, Barbara. "The Flexible Heart of the Home." Places Journal, May 2018.
Phelan, Peggy. Unmarked: The Politics of Performance. New York: Routledge, 1993.
Rawes, Peg. "Housing Biopolitics and Care." In Critical and Clinical Cartographies: Embodiment, Technology, Care, Design. Edited by Andrej Radman and Heidi Sohn. Edinburgh: Edinburgh University Press, 2018.
Sanders, Joel, and Susan Stryker. "Stalled: Gender-Neutral Public Bathrooms." South Atlantic Quarterly 115, no. 4 (2016): 779–88.
Spivak, Gayatri Chakravorty. Can the Subaltern Speak?. Basingstoke: Macmillan, 1988.
Taylor, Keeanga-Yamahtta. How We Get Free: Black Feminism and the Combahee River Collective. Chicago: Haymarket Books, 2017.
Weeks, Kathi. "The Problems with Work." New Labor Forum 23, no. 2 (May 2014): 10–12.

THE NO, NEIN, NIET!!!!! MANIFESTO

The No, Nein, Niet!!!!! manifesto condemns the strategies implemented by a large number of artistic institutions in recent years that have blurred the issue of sexism in art and contemporary culture, and undermined feminist struggles for equality. As a result of those strategies, and despite the fact that for over 30 years 70% of art graduates in the EU have been women, female artists still represent fewer than 20% of those featured in the programmes and collections of museums and art galleries. Such strategies also play a part in the creation and diffusion of an androcentric artistic and cultural history.

The No, Nein, Niet!!!!! manifesto recalls how, in the 1960s and 1970s, the feminist movement launched a new front of action in the form of Feminist Art, which grew on both sides of the Atlantic through intensive dialogue between artists, theorists and activists. This front, which saw women's bodies as a battleground, also declared the discipline of art to be another battlefront, noting that museums and art history systematically excluded female artists.

The No, Nein, Niet!!!!! manifesto insists that if the question, "Have there been great female artists in history?" leads to a critique of patriarchal artistic institutions, in subsequent years another question, "Can art history survive feminism?" will query whether art history and artistic and educational institutions, between which a symbiotic relationship exists, can take on board feminist critiques and demands. Feminist Art, in common with the feminist movement of which it is a part, experienced a golden age which began to decline in the late 1980s; years marked by the institutionalisation of feminism.

The No, Nein, Niet!!!!! manifesto emphasises that Feminist Art maintains that sex as a category structures social issues, the way things are viewed, and language; as well as art as a discipline and its institutions, bringing together aesthetic and political institutions to condemn and fight discrimination against women, and their exploitation and oppression. This manifesto stands with the female writers who view it as the last vanguard of the 20th century; a vanguard whose agenda is being taken up again by new generations of artists, by others in the discipline of art, and by activists and supporters.

The No, Nein, Niet!!!!! manifesto views the discipline of art as an international circuit that affects relationships between local and global settings, cutting across public and private institutions which produce, display and collect art. It invites those who are active within the field of art to practice feminist disobedience.

SAY NO, NEIN, NIET IN THE 21ST CENTURY

> 1. To art that does not question the oppression of women or of other minoritised people because it upholds that oppression.
> To curatorship and writing on the subject of art that obscure the exploitation of women and other minoritised people, because they support that exploitation.
> To museums and art galleries that do nothing to rectify discrimination against

female artists and artists from other minoritised groups, because they themselves engage in that discrimination.

2. To participating in projects involving collaboration with processes that aestheticize social and political issues, and that play a part in consolidating the institutional whitewashing of sexism, LGBTQ-phobia and/ or racism in the discipline of art.
To participating and collaborating in institutional strategies of tokenism, whose visibility peaks around significant dates for feminists such as 8th March or 25th November, because they leave institutionally sexist structures intact. Tokenism consists of including minoritised groups — for example, women — to create the illusion that they are truly equal, thus avoiding accusations of discrimination.
To participating in and organising feminist guided tours of museum collections that fail to reveal the sexist structures of art institutions and their collections.
To promoting a perverse, self-serving synonymy between queerness and feminism that halts or holds back the inclusion of women artists and their work in the collections and programmes of museums and art galleries.

3. To visiting museums and art institutions that, having been turned into flamboyant monuments to contemporary cynicism, put in place whitewashing strategies that conceal their disdain for feminist demands.
To cultural policies that objectify and turn women and other minoritised people into entertainment.

Support for this manifesto is not dependent on being classified as a woman. The principles of equality and respect should be applied and respected by everyone, regardless of their sex/ gender.

Bilbao, 15th November 2018. CONFERENCE ON ART, RESEARCH AND FEMINISMS, Bizkaia Aretoa UPV/EHU (University of the Basque Country)

SIGNATORIES:
Xabier Arakistain, Independent art curator, Bilbao
Lourdes Méndez, Professor of Anthropology of Art, University of the Basque Country, San Sebastian
Txaro Arrazola, Artist and Lecturer in the Faculty of Fine Art, University of the Basque Country, Vitoria-Gasteiz
Andrea Abalia, Artist and Lecturer in the Department of Visual Arts Education, University of the Basque Country, Bilbao
Leticia Gaspar, Artist and Lecturer in the Faculty of Fine Art, University of the Basque Country, Bilbao
David Macho, Artist, Barcelona
Noelia Maeso, Artist and researcher, Bilbao
Lorena Relloso, Artist and researcher, Bilbao
Seila Fernández Arconada, Artist and researcher, Santander
Verónica Fernández, Art postgraduate and researcher, Bilbao
Gurutze Gisasola, Specialist in Educational Support, Bilbao
María José Aranzasti, Art historian and curator, Zarautz